Alonzo Reed

Introductory Language Work

A Simple, Varied, and Pleasing, But Methodical, Series of Exercises in English to

Precede the Study of Technical Grammar

Alonzo Reed

Introductory Language Work
A Simple, Varied, and Pleasing, But Methodical, Series of Exercises in English to Precede the Study of Technical Grammar

ISBN/EAN: 9783744645782

Printed in Europe, USA, Canada, Australia, Japan

Cover: Foto ©Thomas Meinert / pixelio.de

More available books at **www.hansebooks.com**

INTRODUCTORY LANGUAGE WORK

A SIMPLE, VARIED, AND PLEASING,
BUT METHODICAL,
SERIES OF EXERCISES IN ENGLISH
TO PRECEDE THE STUDY OF TECHNICAL GRAMMAR.

BY

ALONZO REED, A.M.,

AUTHOR OF "WORD LESSONS," AND JOINT AUTHOR OF "REED AND KELLOGG'S
LESSONS IN ENGLISH," ETC.

NEW YORK
EFFINGHAM MAYNARD & CO., PUBLISHERS,
771 BROADWAY AND 67 & 69 NINTH STREET.
1891.

LANGUAGE WORK IN THE ELEMENTARY GRADES.

A Talk with Teachers.

Should Language be Taught Directly, or only Incidentally?—Careful and intelligent experiment has of late cleared away much of the fog of conflicting theory and method surrounding the subject of language teaching, so that it is now beginning to take definite form and to receive rational treatment.

The theory that language is best taught indirectly through a series of "information lessons" is giving place to the conviction that the chief business of the language teacher is with the adaptation of the expression to the thought. It is impossible to carry on a course of object lessons and a course of language lessons together and make both consecutive and progressive. One must be sacrificed to the other, and it is invariably the language work that gives way. It is comparatively easy to make a series of object lessons continuous or to fill up the time of recitation with general information, while it is extremely difficult to bring oral language lessons within any well-defined plan or purpose.

That there are forms and principles of language which may be presented at an early age and made to govern the pupils' practice through life, and that such forms and principles should be taught directly, systematically, and persistently, are conclusions now quite generally accepted.

Is Oral Teaching Methodical and Permanent?—The fact that teachers after years of experiment have become dissatisfied with the very uncertain results of oral instruction is evidenced by the growing demand from our best schools for a text-book suitable for the pupils' use and for class-room drill.

Without a drill book in the hands of the pupils there is necessarily a serious loss of time in getting written exercises before the class, and in repeating instruction to bridge over breaks caused by lack of attention or by irregular attendance. But with the best effort of both teacher and class, young pupils find it almost impossible so to hold their oral instruction in memory as to be able to look back over the successive steps and get a bird's-eye view of the different lessons in their proper relations.

A successful teacher will give much oral instruction, and will throw his own personality into his work. The importance of bringing the instructed mind of the teacher into direct contact with the uninstructed mind of the pupil should not be undervalued. But unless oral work is supplemented by a rational text-book, it must lack continuity and permanency. Besides, getting instruction from the printed page is an essential part of language training.

Matter and Method of the Language Book.—The more thoughtful teachers are beginning to question the wisdom of those courses of language study in which spelling, pronunciation, technical grammar, pictures for imaginative stories, poetry for memorizing and paraphrasing, information lessons, and other miscellaneous matter are prescribed, with no line of connection, no beginning, no middle, no end.

Why should the study of our mother tongue be made the one exception to Burke's motto, "Good order is the foundation of all good things"? And is it true that language books must needs be filled with the odds and ends of various subjects because there is so little to be done in the study of language proper?

Spelling and Pronunciation.—Since "language lessons" are supposed to deal mainly with related ideas, why should a language book be interlarded with lessons in pronunciation and spelling, when these subjects are amply provided for in two other text-books of the same grade—the "reader" and the "speller"?

Technical Grammar.—All instruction that aims *chiefly* to lay a foundation for technical grammar is out of place in the primary grades. There are, however, certain grammatical forms that should be brought to the pupils' notice as early as possible, and worked into practice by constant repetition.

Pictures for Stories.—Pictures to aid in imaginative story-writing may, for occasional exercises, serve a useful purpose; but when they are introduced into the language book and kept constantly before the pupils as composition lessons, the story-writing loses the very important element of freshness and surprise. Such exercises are much more interesting and successful if the picture is first presented by the teacher at the hour of recitation. There is danger of overdoing this feature of composition work.

Poetry.—The reproduction of stories found in poems is an exercise of extremely doubtful utility. When we remember that the story is one of the most remote of the poet's purposes, and that the noblest poems of our language drop into insignificance when reduced to "plot" or "argument," it will be seen how positively harmful it must be for the young student to get the impression that his feeble story reproduction is in any sense a measure of the beautiful thought of a great poet.

Concerning the use of poetry for written paraphrase, Laurie says: "A more detestable exercise I do not know. It is an impious and unholy use of pen and ink."* Bain, after quoting one of the best attempts at paraphrasing poetry, remarks: "It has stripped the passage of its poetical beauty, and has not made a good piece of prose. It is an operation without assignable result." †

The translating of poetry into prose by simply changing the order, supplying ellipses, and revoking poetic licenses, is a profitable exercise for grammar grades.

In the primary grades, all pupils able to write should occasionally copy from the blackboard and memorize short selections of poetry. The teacher's chief aim should be to help the pupils to see the beauty of the word-pictures,

---

* "Lectures on Language and Linguistic Method," delivered in the University of Cambridge, England.
† "On Teaching English."

to appreciate the rhythmic flow of the language, and to get into sympathy with the sentiment. Here the text-book can be of little aid. The teacher certainly does not need to be told when and where he can best find opportunity to introduce such general exercises.

Plan of this Book—Observation and Practice.—Extreme reaction from abstract and formal methods has popularized the theory that precision in language comes only from practice, and that the child should constantly be exercised in expressing his own thought in his own language. How progress is to be attained by confining him to the feeble, commonplace expression of his own feeble, commonplace thought does not appear.

Excellence in language is attained through *observation* and *practice*.

In his lecture, "On the Study of Literature," Morley says: "So far as my observation has gone, men will do better if they seek precision by studying carefully and with an open mind and a vigilant eye the models of writing, than by excessive practice of writing on their own account."

Pupils should occasionally write original compositions—frequently, if the teacher can give the individual attention that will make them helpful. It has truly been said that we cannot know that we possess language, or anything else, till we can *use* it. It is equally true that we must acquire language before we can use it.

Distinguished masters and students of style are agreed that good language is got chiefly by the careful study of good models. "Exhaustive observation," says Spencer, "is an element in all great success." This all-important feature of language training has been most strangely neglected.

In the following lessons will be found a connected and progressive series of exercises in *observation* and *practice*. Most of the drill work will be found under the two heads, *What to See* and *What to Do*.

The Sentence and the Paragraph.—The sentence, the unit of language, is examined with regard to its meaning, its written form, and its relation to the paragraph.

Very early in the work the paragraph is presented as a part, or division, of the story, and its content and its form are carefully noted.

Pupils are led to use the imagination in making word-pictures from outlines—dressing up the bare statements of a story or a description by adding appropriate helping words and phrases. They are taught to combine and arrange these statements in various ways, so as to secure a natural and easy flow of thought. Their attention is called to the importance of keeping up interest and of holding the most important things for the final outcome.

Chief Parts and their Helpers.—In connection with this work, and as an essential part of it, the sentence is examined for its chief parts. The forms and the relations of these parts are taught by easy, informal exercises in *seeing* and *doing*.

Around the chief words the pupils are taught to group the different helping words and phrases, not as a work of formal analysis, but as a simple process of noting what words do and mean as they are used in the sentence.

There is nothing within the whole range of language study more profitable than this. When the pupil has acquired the habit of noting the chief words of a sentence at a glance, he has laid the most solid foundation for regulating his own language and for observing the language of others.

Cobbett says that half of all grammatical errors come from not ascertaining the nominative. But going beyond the mere matter of grammatical correctness, this work of noting what words and phrases do furnishes the only intelligent means of learning how to get ideas into good arrangement—a difficulty, as Bain suggests, greater than all other difficulties put together.

The Thought and the Language of the Exercises.—Although these lessons deal primarily with expression, the expression is considered in its concrete relation to the thought. The aim has been to present such exercises as will incidentally convey information and stimulate original thought. Some of the lessons designed for composition work will lead the pupil into sympathy with nature, and with what is noble and heroic in character.

The language employed is intended to be in advance of the pupil's own language. The child enjoys the effort of reaching up for what is a little above him, but is disgusted with attempts to talk down to his level.

Common Errors.—Special effort has been made to aid pupils in forming correct habits of language where there is most danger of falling into bad habits. Forms liable to misuse are noticed incidentally till the development of the work gives opportunity for treating them thoroughly.

Frequent repetition of correct forms, and reasons reached through simple processes of observation, are both employed to secure right habits. The sentences given for repetition are, for obvious reasons, colloquial, rather than literary, in their character.

Abstract Terms.—Abstract and technical terms are here generally avoided. They frighten young children, and make the natural and easy seem unnatural and difficult.

Letter-writing.—Letter-writing receives extended and careful treatment. Models are given for copying. Important points are emphasized and different forms impressed, by searching observation lessons, and for everything thus taught the pupil is held responsible in the dictation exercises.

Opportunity for Work.—As a means of getting thought, as well as of expressing thought, systematic training in the observation and practice of language cannot begin too early nor continue too persistently. There certainly can be no lack of legitimate work for the language teacher.

It is not claimed for this series of exercises that they will enable the pupil to overcome all the difficulties of language. When we have put the young child's feet in the right path and given him an impulse in the right direction, we have done much. A. R.

NEW YORK, *June*, 1891.

To the Teacher.

SUGGESTIONS ON THE USE OF THE FOLLOWING LESSONS.

Exercises under the Head of "What to See" may be read in the class, one pupil reading a question and another giving the answer, and so on. The remarks found with these questions should also be read and discussed. The teacher should see that every form or principle in the illustrative exercises is impressed. The pupils may be stimulated to closer observation by being assured that, after closing the books, they are to write similar sentences.

Copied exercises may be exchanged, and corrected from the book by the pupils.

Oral Composition Lessons should generally precede the written. Each pupil should be called upon to tell some part of the story, or to put in different language what has been told by another. The clearest and neatest of these sentences should be put on the board.

The teacher should use every effort to secure a smooth flow of thought from one sentence to another, an easy transition from one paragraph to another, and a natural outcome for the whole story or description.

The Correction of Written Compositions is most effective when done in the presence of the pupils at the time of recitation. The teacher, certainly, has no right to unfit himself for his duties in the classroom by giving all his leisure hours to the correction of compositions.

While the pupils are writing their exercises, the teacher can pass from one to another, making corrections and helpful suggestions. The slower pupils may need to rewrite their work after the recitation hour.

Some of the compositions should be read in the class. General errors should be corrected and explained by the aid of the blackboard.

If the work of one "Lesson" cannot be well done in the period for recitation, let the "Lesson" be divided.

For Additional Exercises in Composition the teacher may read to the class short stories or selections. As each paragraph is read, the pupils should tell what it is about. The outline thus obtained should be put on the board. The whole selection may then be read the second time, and the pupils may reproduce it in paragraphs to correspond with the outline.

It is better, for obvious reasons, that these selections for reproduction should not be in the pupils' language books.

Sentences to Guard against Common Errors are given in the full and correct form for repetition. Thus the eye, the tongue, and the ear are trained together. For tests, these exercises may be put on the board or dictated with blanks to be filled.

By questions and various devices the teacher should create occasion for continuing the use of those expressions in which he finds his pupils liable to err. He should, with unremitting vigilance, correct all errors made by the pupils in conversation or in recitation. Reasons and references to the text-book should be given as soon as the pupils are prepared for them.

INTRODUCTORY LANGUAGE WORK.

PART FIRST.

To the Teacher.—It is important for the teacher to see that the following lessons form a connected course of instruction, that the relation of a topic or a principle to what precedes or follows determines its place of introduction, and that, instead of formal **reviews**, **composition** and **observation exercises** are so designed that the different principles presented are kept in constant application.

The four different kinds of sentences and the three terminal marks are introduced in the first ten lessons as a necessary foundation for intelligent composition work. As subsequent exercises repeat and continue the instruction given in these lessons, to extend this introductory work beyond a simple and clear presentation would be bad economy.

LESSON I.

Statements — Capitals — Period.

To the Teacher.—If the pupils are allowed to copy this outline of the ant, and to talk about it and about the statements below, it will give a keener interest to these exercises. A valuable oral lesson is here suggested.

The observation exercises added to these lessons may be read with the pupils in an easy, conversational way. Lead the pupils to talk freely, but to a purpose.

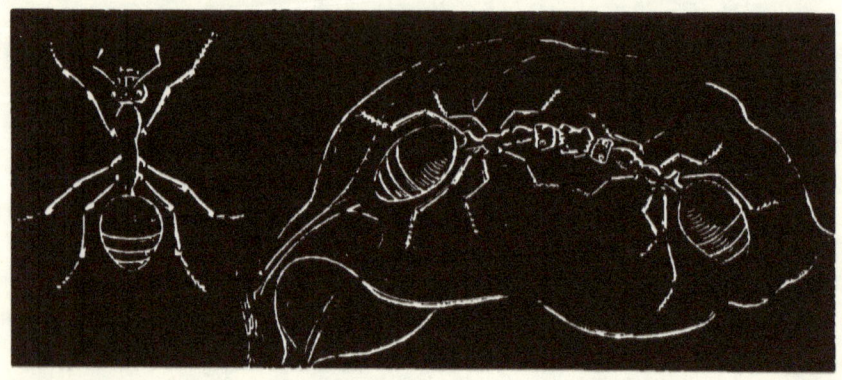

Copy the following very carefully:—

Ants build neat homes.
Some ants are farmers.
Baby ants have nurses.
Some ants keep slaves.
These insects are very wise.

What to See.—The first group of words above begins with what kind of letter?

Describe the mark after the last word of this group.

You may call this mark a **Period.**

Tell how each of the other groups begins and ends.

Does each group make sense by itself?

Leave out *build* from the first sentence, and then see whether it will make sense.

Will it make sense if you leave out *ants?*

Will it make sense if you leave out the last two words?

Dictation Exercises.

To the Teacher.—After copying these sentences, the pupils may turn over their slates and write the same from dictation.

Original Statements.

Each pupil may write one sentence of his own. Such sentences will probably be suggested by the oral exercise.

LESSON II.

Statements — Capitals — Period.

To the Teacher.—The statements below, with the cut in the preceding lesson, will suggest an oral exercise.

Copy these lines very neatly :—

This little body has three parts. All insects have three parts. Ants are busy creatures. They run about on six legs.

What to See.—How many periods have you just copied ?
How many groups of words making complete sense ?
With what kind of letter does each group begin ?
What do you find at the end of each group ?

A group of words making complete sense is a Sentence.

In writing several sentences together we must show where one ends and another begins.

EXERCISE.

This little body has three parts all insects have three parts ants are busy creatures they run about on six legs.

What to See.—Can you read the sentences in these lines as easily as you can the same sentences at the beginning of this lesson ?
Find all the differences.
How may the different sentences be kept apart ?
Of what use is the period ?
How do capitals help ?
How do we show where one sentence ends and another begins ?

Dictation Exercise.

To the Teacher.—These sentences may be written from dictation and then compared with the book for correction.

Original Statements.

Each pupil may write a sentence of his own.

LESSON III.

Statements — Capitals — Period.

Copy the sentences below and notice all about them :—

The ant's legs are joined to the middle part.

On its head are two feel-ers.

Hundreds of ants live in one house.

In these houses are many rooms and halls.

What to See.—How many sentences have you copied ?
How do you find out ?
How many lines in the first sentence ?
Which line begins farther to the right than the other ?
How does the first line in each of the other sentences begin ?
Notice that the first syllable of *feel-ers* is on one line, and the second syllable on the next line.

It would be wrong to divide a syllable.

Notice the little mark after *feel-*.

This shows that the word will be finished on the next line.

Additional Work.

To the Teacher.—The pupils may give orally the facts related in the preceding lessons. They may be led to vary their statements and to join them into connected stories.

Some of the best sentences may be put on the blackboard or the slates.

Attention may be called to the apostrophe in these exercises, without attempting a full explanation.

Dictation Exercise.

Let the pupils write the script sentences from dictation.

LESSON IV.

Questions — Question Mark — Capitals.

To the Teacher.—An oral lesson on the spider is here suggested. The outline of the spider is made simple for copying.

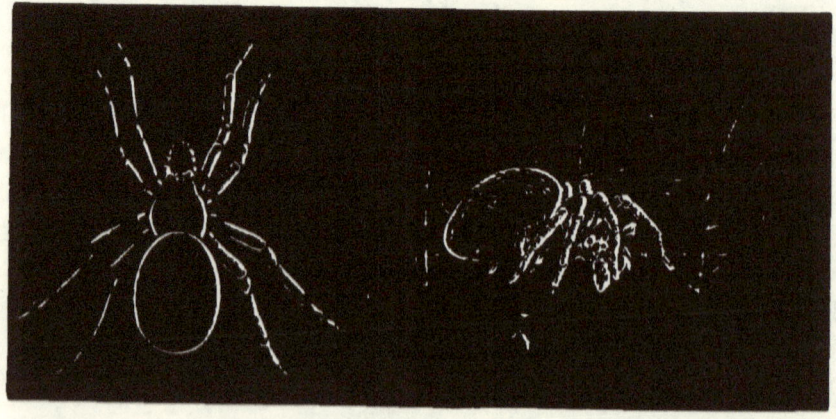

QUESTIONS—QUESTION MARK—CAPITALS.

Copy the five lines below :—

Do spiders work?
What can they do?
What do spiders eat?
How many legs has a spider?
An ant has how many legs?

What to See.—Does the first group of words above make sense ?

What do we call a group of words that makes sense ?

Does the first sentence *tell* us something about spiders ?

What does it do ?

What does the second sentence do ?

Tell what each of the others does.

Then each of these sentences is a *question*.

The little crooked **Question Mark** at the end helps to show this.

In the sentences before this lesson we tell, or *state*, something—make **Statements**.

In these sentences we *ask* about something—make **Questions**.

With what kind of letter does each question above begin ?

What mark is put at the end of each question ?

Dictation and Original Work.

To the Teacher.—The questions found in script may be written from dictation.

Pupils may write one or more sentences of their own.

LESSON V.

Questions and Statements — Question Mark — Period — Capitals.

Copy the sentences below :—

Do spiders have wings?
Some ants have wings.
Is the spider's body soft?
It is in two parts.
Do you see the spider's eight legs?

What to See.—Which of the groups above are sentences ?

Which may be called statements because they state, or tell, something ?

Which are questions ?

With what kind of letter does each of these sentences begin ?

Does each end in the same way?
What do the statements end with?
What do the questions end with?
Make the *question mark* neatly.

Dictation and Original Work.

To the Teacher.—The script sentences may be dictated. Pupils may change orally one kind to the other. Some of the pupils' own sentences may be written. (See suggestion concerning the apostrophe, Lesson III.)

LESSON VI.

Questions and Statements — Question Mark — Period — Capitals.

Copy the sentences below :—

Are the spider's legs all on the front part? The hind part is large and round. It carries the glue for making silken thread.

Is the spider pretty? Some spiders have rich colors.

What to See. — How many sentences do you find in the first five lines?

How do you find out?

Will the first make sense if we leave out *are?*

How is the first separated from the second?

From the "exercise" in Lesson II. what did you learn about the use of the period?

Can the question mark, as well as the period, help to show where one sentence ends and another begins?

How many sentences in the last two lines?

Tell how each of the five sentences begins and ends.

All the five sentences are about the spider. In the first three we talk about the spider's two parts, so we may begin one sentence right after another and make of the three one group.

In the last two sentences we talk about the spider's looks, so we may make one group of these.

How are these groups of sentences separated?

What two lines begin farther to the right than the others?

Notice the little mark — hyphen — after *mak-* at the end of the fourth line. It separates two syllables. (See Lesson III.)

Dictation Exercises.

To the Teacher. — In dictating these exercises let special attention be given to the way in which the groups are separated.

The length of the pupils' lines should correspond to the width of the paper or slate used, rather than to the copy.

LESSON VII.

Joining Sentences.

Copy the following :—

The spider's legs are all on the front part of the body. The hind part, which is large and round, carries the glue for making silken thread. The spider is not pretty in shape, but it often has very rich colors.

What to See.—The sentences in Lesson VI. have here been changed a little, and some of them have been linked together. Tell all you can about what has happened in making the new groups.

Additional Work.

To the Teacher.—Pupils may be encouraged to point out most of the changes in these sentences. Guard against attempting too much, or what is technical. Similar experiments may be made with other preceding lessons. Pupils may join the sentences orally. Some of the best may be commended and placed on the board for copying.

The form of the *paragraph*, the use of the *apostrophe* and of the *hyphen*, the form of the word *I* (Lessons VIII., X., etc.), and the use of the comma to denote a slight break or pause, may be taught without formal presentation, fuller treatment being anticipated.

LESSON VIII.

Exclamations — Exclamation Mark — Capitals.

Copy the lines below :—

How the wind blows!
What clouds of dust sweep along!
How dark it grows!
How the woods roar!
What strange sounds I hear!

What to See.—Do you ever make such sentences as these when you are excited ?

When you are surprised or afraid, do you ever *exclaim?*

What you say when you exclaim is called an **Exclamation.**

What are these five *exclamations* all about?
Does each exclamation here make sense?
Then what shall we call each?
With what kind of letter does each sentence begin?
Learn to make the **Exclamation Mark** at the end very neatly.
What does *I* mean in the last sentence?
Notice that this word *I* is a capital letter.

Dictation.

To the Teacher.—The pupils should write these sentences from dictation.

LESSON IX.

Commands — Period — Capitals.

Copy the lines below:—

Listen to the large rain-drops.
Now run into the house.
Shut the door.
Put the windows down.
See the people run.

What to See.—Does each group of words here make sense?

Then what may each group be called?

Are they exclamations?

Do they ask about anything?

Do they simply tell, or state, what something does?

They tell some one to do something.

They are **Commands.**

How does each *command* begin and end?

Read the last sentence as if you greatly enjoyed seeing the people run.

Now write it with an exclamation mark at the end.

This shows that the sentence is no longer intended as a command, but merely as an exclamation.

What are all these sentences about?

What are those in Lesson VIII. about?

LESSON X.

Different Kinds of Sentences.

Copy the sentences below :—

The clouds are breaking.
Come out on the piazza.
Children are wading in the pools.

Do the ducks enjoy the rain?

How the shadows skim over the meadows!

Where shall I look for a rainbow?

What to See.—What is the first sentence called?
Does the second tell some one to do something?
Then what kind of sentence is it?
Remember that a command is not always stern. It may be a gentle request or an invitation.
What mark at the end of a statement?
What mark at the end of a command?
Read the exclamation.
What mark at the end of the exclamation?
Read the two questions.
What mark at the end of each question?
What does *I* in the last sentence mean?
This word is always written as a capital letter.

Dictation Exercises.

To the Teacher.—Let the pupils write the script sentences from dictation.

LESSON XI.

Putting Sentences Together.

To the Teacher.—The pupils may read aloud the talk below, and make up the story orally.

The order in which these things should be told requires attention.

Some of the best of the changed, connected, or original sentences should be written.

THE STORY OF A SUMMER SHOWER.

What to Do.—If you will read over the sentences copied in the three preceding lessons, you will find that they make a short story about *A Summer Shower*.

The sentences are quite short, and so the story seems rather broken.

Perhaps you can change some of these sentences and link some together so as to make the story read more smoothly.

Notice how the sentences of Lesson VI. were put together in Lesson VII.

In writing two sentences that you have linked together, you will need but one capital; as,

The wind blows, and the woods roar.

Notice the comma between the two statements.

As you have seen many showers, and have noticed things not mentioned here, you may fill in and finish the story.

LESSON XII.

Original Work.

What to Do.—Think of some hard shower that you have seen, and be prepared to tell your teacher and your class about it.

We will give you here some—

HINTS.

Where were you when the storm came up? What did you do? How did the sky, clouds, trees, grass, grain, leaves, papers, hats, birds, chickens, geese, horses, cattle, people, etc., look or act before and during the storm? What happened after the storm? What damage was done? What good was done?

To the Teacher.—Nature in her varying phases and moods will ever be an unfailing source of interest to a child.

The teacher of language may secure many original and thoughtful exercises in composition by leading the pupils to recall their own observations of the things and the processes about them.

In the exercise suggested above the pupils should not be allowed to talk at random. Their best sentences should be noted. These they should write.

Perhaps the combining and correcting of these may require another recitation.

LESSON XIII.

A Study of Sentences.

EXERCISE.

1. An ant went to get a drink.
2. It fell into the water.
3. Poor thing!
4. A dove dropped a branch into the water.
5. The ant got out.

What to See.—How many sentences above?

Poor thing! does not make complete sense.

We do not always make sentences when we exclaim.

What kind of feeling do these two words seem to show?

As this exclamation is by itself, we begin it with a capital.

Read these lines together.

Does not our story seem to go jumping along?

Do you not think these groups of words could run together more smoothly?

And do you not think the statements rather bare?

Could we not make our story better by dressing them up a little?

Now you may tell the story so as to interest a younger brother or sister.

To the Teacher.—Let the pupils close their books and try their skill. They will need guidance. Some of the best work may be written. The word *ant* above suggests exercises on the homonyms—

ant, aunt.

LESSON XIV.

Dressing Up Sentences and Putting Them Together.

Copy the lines below:—

The Ant and the Dove.

One hot day an ant went down to a brook to drink; but, poor thing! it fell into the water.

A dove saw it, and dropped a branch into the stream.

The little ant clung to the branch, and so got safe to land.

To the Teacher.—If too much matter for one lesson is found here, some of the observation exercises may be used, with an exercise in dictation, for another lesson.

What to See.—Now read this story as given in Lesson XIII.

Which is the smoother and better way of telling the story?

Why?

In dressing up the first sentence, what three words are put in to tell *when* the ant went?

What words are put in to tell *where* the ant went to drink?

Do you think it makes a story more interesting to tell when and where the things happened?

What word seems to join the first two sentences?

Leave out this word, and see that the period is then needed after *drink*.

In this second writing of the story, what two things do we say the dove did?

We make the story better by putting in *saw it*, for we then show that the dove helped the ant purposely.

In the last two lines what two things do we say the ant did?

Here we have bettered the story by telling *how* the ant got out.

What do we tell last?

Is not this the most interesting thing?

We should always try to keep the best part of the story for the last.

We find this story has three parts :—

        1st, *The ant's accident.*
        2d, *The dove's help.*
        3d, *The ant's escape.*

Now see whether you can tell why we made three groups of the script lines.

How are the breaks between these lines made?

What do you notice about the first word of each group?

To the Teacher.—The pupils' attention may be called to the comma and the semicolon. To copy them correctly may be sufficient here. Possibly the pupils may be made to see that these marks separate the parts of the sentences, and show when the sense requires a shorter or longer pause.

Few rules for punctuation should be given till the pupil is familiar with the analysis of sentences.

LESSON XV.

Dressing Up Sentences and Putting Them Together.

EXERCISE.

1. A man put up his gun to shoot the dove.
2. The ant bit the man's heel.
3. Bang! went the gun.
4. The dove was not hurt.
5. The ant helped the dove.
6. The dove helped the ant.
7. Shall we help each other?

To the Teacher.—The time of one recitation could profitably be spent in letting the pupils work the sentences above into good story form without the aid of the script exercise.

Copy the following :—

The Ant and the Dove.

Two or three days after, the ant saw a man put up his gun to shoot the poor dove.

The ant crept up and bit the man in the heel. The gun went off, but the dove was not hurt.

So the ant and the dove helped each other. Shall we, too, try to help each other?

What to See.—With the above read the other part of the same story as told at the beginning of Lesson XIV.

In dressing up the first sentence, what words have been put in to tell when this thing happened?

If it were not for the comma before *the,* one in reading

our story might put the words *after the ant* together, and not get our meaning so easily.

Now look at the rest of this story, and find what has been added to the sentences at the beginning of this lesson, and how they have been put together.

In this story, do the ant and the dove think and act like persons?

This is the way animals do in *fables*.

Are fables entirely true?

Fables should teach us something.

Read the last group of script lines, and then tell what this fable teaches.

We will strip this story down and find what it is framed on:—

   1st, *The dove's danger.*
   2d, *The ant's help.*
   3d, *What the fable teaches.*

Now tell why the script lines are in three groups.

To the Teacher.—In using these exercises, the teacher will, of course, study the capacity of the children, and give more help, or less help, than he finds here, according to circumstances.

The idea of the paragraph and its form should be carefully noted. Reading easy paragraphs, and telling, in the fewest words, what each is about, is an excellent practice.

Special attention should be called to the words—

two, to, and *too,*

which are in the script lines. Secure their correct spelling and use. Perhaps no other words are more misused.

A GATHERING UP.

To the Teacher.—We do not offer the following as formal rules and definitions. We should not hold the pupils to an exact repetition of the language here given.

A group of words making complete sense is a **Sentence.**

A sentence used to tell, or state, something is a **Statement.**

A sentence used to ask is a **Question.**

A sentence used to show feeling or excitement is an **Exclamation.**

A sentence used to tell or request some one to do something is a **Command.**

A **Period** *is placed at the end of a statement or a command.*

A **Question Mark** *is placed at the end of a question.*

An **Exclamation Mark** *is placed at the end of an exclamation.*

Every sentence should begin with a **Capital Letter.**

A story made up of very short sentences sounds rather jerky.

To make a story read smoothly, we often link two or more sentences together.

There is danger of making our sentences too long.

In writing a story, the sentences should be in groups (or **paragraphs**), each group telling one part, or division, of the story.

The **hyphen** is used at the end of a line where a word is divided. (See Lessons III., VI., etc.)

A syllable should not be divided.

Things Noticed in Passing.

The *apostrophe* and *s* (*'s*) joined to a name show that it is a helping word telling *whose;* as, *ant's legs, spider's body.* (See Lessons III. and V.)

The word *I* should always be a capital letter. (See Lessons VIII. and X.)

LESSON XVI.

Statements — Chief Words.

Copy the lines below :—

Bees buzz.
Bees work all day.
Up go four wings.
Six little legs hang down.
Away goes the little body.
Flowers open their cups.

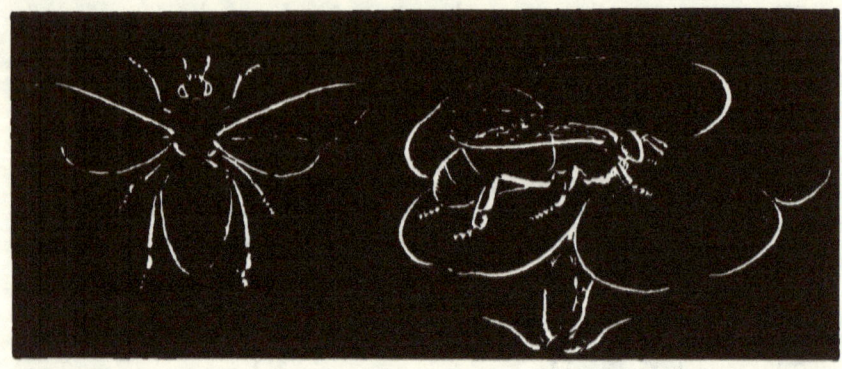

What to See.—Is each group of words at the beginning of this lesson a sentence?

To make complete sense we must say something about something.

In the first sentence, what do we say something about?

What do we say about them?

Find in the second sentence two words that will make sense by themselves.

These are the **chief words**,* the others are helpers.

---

* We can not support the theory that the sentence must first be divided into only two parts—the *entire subject* and the *entire predicate*.

Except as a summing up, we find comparatively little practical good resulting from such work. When the words are all in their natural order, the process is easy, but mechanical.

When some of the words and phrases are transposed, as happens in many of the simplest sentences (1–4, Lesson IV.; 3 and 5, Lesson XVI.; 6, Lesson XVII., etc.), the pupil is compelled first to find his chief words and then to group their helpers around them. If taught to do this at the beginning, his work will be more intelligently done.

Besides, the training of the eye to see the two chief words of a sentence at a glance is of the greatest utility at all times. Such training is a guard against a large part of the errors into which a writer is liable to fall.

In the third sentence we say something about wings.
Find one word that tells what wings do.
In the fourth sentence we say something about legs.
Find one word that tells what legs do.
In the fifth sentence we say something about body.
Find one word that tells what the body does.
In the last sentence we say something about flowers.
Find one word that tells what flowers do.
Now read together the two *chief words* of each sentence.
If in the third or the fifth sentence we wish to show a little more feeling or excitement, we can put an exclamation mark at the end.
In the second sentence what two words tell how long bees work?
In the third, what word tells how many wings?
What word tells where the wings go?

To the Teacher.—We give above three questions to aid in distinguishing the helping words from the chief words.

We believe that any pupil who can read intelligently in the Second Reader will answer such questions with interest if technical terms are avoided, and simple, familiar language is used. He need not know that he is "analyzing." He will like to tell *what his words are for.*

Pupils may here be tested on the spelling and use of—

bee and *be.*

Additional Work.

The sentences in script and the cut, at the beginning of this lesson, will furnish material for oral composition.

Some of the pupils' work may be dictated for writing.

LESSON XVII.

Statements — Chief Words — Names.

Copy the sentences below :—

The bee <u>plunges</u> into the flowers.

The little creature <u>drinks</u> from their cups.

Their yellow dust <u>fills</u> her baskets.

The baskets <u>are</u> on her legs.

Her velvet coat <u>shines</u> in the sun.

At night the busy worker <u>flies</u> to her home.

What to See. — How many sentences above? How do you tell?

To make a sentence we *name* something, and then *say* something about it.

In these sentences we have drawn a line under (*underlined*) the word that *tells*.

You may pick out the other chief word, the *name* of the thing we tell about. (To get this name put *what* before the word underlined and answer your question with one word, in this way: *What plunges? Bee plunges.*)

Read together the two chief words of each sentence.

You see that the two chief words do not always make full sense by themselves.

Find those that you think do make full sense.

These six sentences may be taken together for one story.

What are they all about?

Then what is the subject of our composition?

In these sentences we use three different names for the same insect. Find them.

In the third sentence we tell about dust.

What do we tell about in the fourth?

What do we tell about in the fifth?

Taking each sentence as a short composition, we may call the name of the thing we tell about the **Subject** of the sentence.

This, you see, is not always the same as the subject of the whole composition.

Additional Lessons.

To the Teacher.—For another lesson let the pupils read the script sentences of Lessons XVI. and XVII. together, and work the whole into oral compositions.

Some of these altered and combined sentences may be written in the form of short paragraphs.

Helping Words.

To bring out the helping words we suggest such questions as the following :—

In the first sentence what three words together tell where the bee plunges?
In the third, what word tells the color of the dust?
What does *on her legs* tell?
In the fifth, what word tells whose coat?
What does *her* mean?
What does *velvet* tell?
What does *in the sun* tell?
In the sixth, what word tells what kind of worker?
What tells where the worker flies?
When does the worker fly to her home?

LESSON XVIII.

Chief Words — Names — Capitals.

Copy the sentences below and notice all capitals :—

Our longest river <u>flows</u> southerly.

The Mississippi <u>rises</u> in Minnesota.

In 1492 Columbus <u>sailed</u> westward.

This brave sailor once <u>lived</u> in Italy.

What to See.—In each of these sentences we have underlined the word that tells. You may put *what* or *who* before this word and find the other chief word, the name of the thing we tell about.

Which of these chief names begin with a capital?

Which begin with a small letter?

Many streams of water have the same name, *river*, because they are alike.

Are many streams called *Mississippi* because they are alike?

Many persons are called *sailors* because they are alike in what they do.

Are many persons called *Columbus* because they are alike?

Things that are alike, or of one kind, we put together and give them all one common name, as, *river*. But each river has also its own particular name, as, *Mississippi*.

Find in these sentences two names each belonging to a particular place.

How does each **particular name** begin?

How does each **common name** begin?

Additional Work.

To the Teacher.—We believe that, at the very beginning of written language work, children can be taught to note, in an easy and natural way, what the different words and phrases do in their sentences. Such work should not be separated from that of determining the meaning of the sentence and of the words that compose it.

Noting the uses of words and phrases will soon become a habit. Such a habit will be a powerful aid to clear writing and intelligent reading.

Questions to bring out such uses should be varied and informal. All technical distinctions and close classifications should here be scrupulously avoided.

We suggest such as the following :—

In the first sentence what helping word tells whose river ?
What does *our* mean here ?
How does *southerly* help ?
In Minnesota does what ?
What helps *sailed* by telling when ?
What does *westward* do ?
What word tells what kind of sailor ?
What helps *lived* by telling where ?
If a question does not bring out the right answer, try a more suggestive one.

Dictation.

The sentences in script may be written from dictation.

LESSON XIX.

Names — Capitals.

ORAL WORK.

Give a name that belongs to many persons of the same kind.

Give a name that belongs to one particular person.

The common name *village* is given to many places that are alike.

Give the particular names of villages near you.

The common name *dog* is given to a large class of animals.

Give the particular name of some dog, cat, horse, or other pet animal.

The common name *city* belongs to a whole class of places.

Give the particular names of some large cities.

What kind of names are *boat, kite, sled, doll?*

Can you give the particular name of a boat, kite, sled, or doll?

To the Teacher.—Some of these names may be put on the board for copying.

Copy the names below:—

Arthur, man, farmer, Daniel, George, Isaac, William, boy, soldier, Blanche, Edith, woman, Eliza, lady, Lydia, Victoria, doctor, queen, Philadelphia, town, city.

What to See.—Which of these names are given to many persons or places that are alike?

Which are particular names?

What do you here learn about capitals?

Notice that these words, when written in lines, are separated by the comma.

LESSON XX.

Chief Words — Names — Capitals.

Two or More Words in One Name.

Copy the sentences below:—

Washington lived in Virginia.

George Washington marched with Braddock.

General George Washington led our army.

Our first president died at Mount Vernon.

What to See.—How many sentences do you find here? How do you tell?

Notice that in these sentences we have underlined the name of the one we talk about (our subject).

Notice that in the second sentence the chief name is made up of two words.

In the third sentence the chief name is made up of three words.

In the fourth sentence *president* is the chief name; *our* and *first* are only helpers, showing which president we are talking about.

Find in each sentence the chief word telling what the person did.

Which of these chief names belong each to one particular person?

Which may belong to any person holding the highest office in our country?

Look at these names and tell what you learn about capitals.

Find among the helping words in these sentences three particular names.

Tell how many words in each, and how each word begins.

Additional Work—Dictation.

To the Teacher.—Let the script sentences be written from dictation.

The offices of the helping words may be brought out by such questions as—

 What does *in Virginia* tell?
 What did Washington lead?
 Where did he die?
 What does *at Mount Vernon* tell?

LESSON XXI.

Names — Capitals.

EXERCISES FOR WRITING.

Write your own full name.
Write the full names of two boys and two girls.
Write the names of two great men.
Mention three states whose names have each two words.
Mention three cities whose names have each two words.
Give the names of three lakes.
Give the names of three ranges of mountains.
Write the twelve names you have given.
Begin each word in each of these names with a capital

LESSON XXII.

Statements — Chief Parts.

EXERCISE.

1. A family of kittens were playing.
2. The mother had lain down.
3. She was watching her kittens.
4. A hawk saw them.
5. He had been looking for a breakfast.
6. A kitten was seized.

STATEMENTS—CHIEF PARTS.

What to See.—Notice in each sentence a straight line under the first chief part, and a waving line under the second chief part.

You will see that the other words are only helpers.

In the first sentence what little phrase of two words tells what kind of family?

In the third what word tells what the cat was watching?

In the fourth what word tells what the hawk saw?

What does *she* mean in the third sentence?

What does *them* mean in the fourth?

What does *he* mean in the fifth?

You know that in these short compositions, or sentences, which we have been making, the name of the thing we speak about is called our *subject*.

Now we need a name for the chief part that tells or says something.

Let us call it the **verb**.

Tell how many words in each of the six verbs.

When you read the six sentences together, do you think they make a smooth, well-finished story?

Do they seem to limp along?

If you will close your book and picture these things to yourself, you can make a better story.

To the Teacher.—The word *verb* is not introduced here to lay a foundation for grammar, but to avoid confusing expressions.

Children will soon learn, without formal instruction, to put the parts of a compound verb together.

In the **oral** work here suggested encourage the pupils to make clear pictures in simple, flowing language.

LESSON XXIII.

Finishing and Joining Sentences.

Copy the two paragraphs below:—

What Happened to a Kitten.

One bright, sunny spring morning a family of kittens were playing about the door of a farmhouse. The mother had lain down, and was watching the playful tricks of her happy kittens.

A large hawk, which had been searching all morning for his breakfast, saw them. Like an arrow he darted upon one of the kittens.

What to See.—Compare the first sentence in Lesson XXII. with the first sentence here.

Do you think that what has been added makes the story better?

Why?

When were the family of kittens playing?

Where were they playing?

Can you tell how the second and third sentences of Lesson XXII. are here changed and put together?

What do we here say the mother was watching?

We want to make this part of the picture as bright, happy, and peaceful as possible before the hawk comes in.

This will make the other part darker in contrast.

See how we have put together the fourth and fifth sentences of Lesson XXII.

We have put the fifth in the middle of the fourth.

Which and *he* both mean *hawk.*

Which binds the sentences together.

Try *he* or *hawk* in place of *which,* and see whether the sentences will flow together easily.

Have you ever seen an arrow drop from above?

How does *like an arrow* help?

Can you see any reason for these lines being in two groups?

To the Teacher.—Such work as is suggested here may be made intensely interesting to children. They will be delighted to learn how to make good stories, or clear, bright word pictures.

These exercises may be extended, varied, and, if necessary, simplified.

Lead the pupils to see clearly how the story is improved by the phrase at the beginning and the one at the end of the first sentence, and by the comparison in the last. Let them suggest other changes.

Let them see how the two sentences are combined in the second period by dropping one subject and making *mother* the subject of both verbs.

Let the pupils see that the commas show where slight breaks or pauses are made in the sentences.

The matter of grouping into paragraphs should be emphasized.

Dictation Lesson.

The paragraphs above may be dictated, and then compared with the book and corrected by the pupils.

LESSON XXIV.

Statements — Chief Parts.

EXERCISE.

1. The mother sprang upon the hawk.
2. A fierce battle was fought.
3. Finally the hawk was killed.
4. The cat had lost one eye.
5. She was covered with blood.
6. Her kitten had been hurt.
7. She licked its wounds.

What to See.—You will find a waving line under the chief part that tells (the verb).

Put *what* before each verb and find the subject.

Read together each subject and its verb.

How many words in each verb?

What phrase of three words tells where the mother sprang?

What word tells what kind of battle was fought?

What tells when the hawk was killed?

What had the cat lost?

What does *she* mean?

What does *her* mean?

What does *its* mean?

Try your skill in making a connected story from these sentences.

LESSON XXV.

Finishing and Joining Sentences.

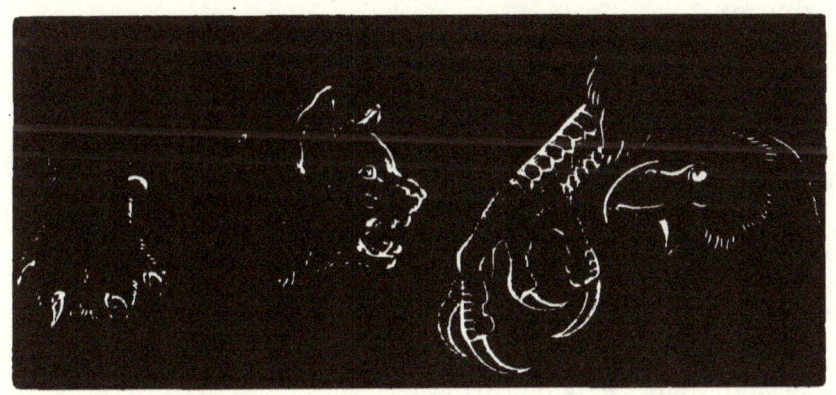

Copy these three paragraphs :—

THE RESCUE BY THE MOTHER.

The mother saw the danger of her little one, and sprang at once upon the hawk.

A long and fierce battle was fought, but at last the hawk was killed.

Though the cat had lost one eye and was covered with blood, she first ran to her kitten and licked its wounds.

What to See.—What words have here been added to the first sentence of Lesson XXIV.?

How do these words help the story?

What has been done with the next two sentences of Lesson XXIV.?

The other sentences are here all linked together.

We dropped *she*, and linked *had lost* and *was covered* by using *and*.

What other changes do you find?

What do you think about them?

As the story is now told, does it appear that the cat cared more for the kitten than for herself?

Though helps to keep the last group of lines together.

Try to stop at *eye* or at *blood* and see whether *though* will let you.

You have seen that *but* and *and* also help in putting together some parts of this story.

Additional Lessons.

To the Teacher.—The pupils should see why five paragraphs are made of this whole story.

Such a skeleton as the following may be put on the board:—

THE CAT AND THE HAWK.
A Happy Family.
A Kitten Seized.
The Mother to the Rescue.
The Battle.
The Mother's Love.

This will show what each paragraph is about, and help the pupil to understand why the sentences are grouped.

The skeleton above may serve as an aid in telling the story orally.

The story may be varied indefinitely. The scene may be changed, the incidents of the battle may be given, etc.

Children may tell of any bird or other animal that has shown great devotion to its young.

What fathers and mothers have done and suffered for their children will furnish excellent matter for short oral and written compositions.

The written work should grow out of the oral story telling.

The weapons of the cat and the hawk, pictured at the beginning of this lesson, will furnish matter for another composition.

LESSON XXVI.

Sentences — Chief Parts.

Words that Take the Place of Names.

EXERCISE.

1. John has spaded the garden.
2. He is making the beds.
3. Fannie will sow some seeds.
4. She has been waiting for a warm day.
5. The honeysuckle has been neatly trained.
6. It is showing green buds.
7. The rose bushes must now be trimmed.
8. They will soon spring into life.
9. You may plant the lilies.
10. In the evening I will sprinkle the garden.
11. Who will destroy the weeds?

What to See.—In these sentences we have drawn a waving line under the second chief part (the verb).

Put *who* or *what* before each verb and find the chief name, or subject.

Read each subject and its verb together.

How many words in each verb?

What does *he* mean in the second sentence?

Can this little word take the place of any man's or boy's name?

In the fourth sentence what name does *she* take the place of?

Can *she* take the place of any woman's or girl's name?

In the sixth sentence what does *it* take the place of?

In the eighth sentence what does *they* mean?

How do you find what *he, she, it,* and *they* mean here?

In the ninth sentence what does *you* mean?

In the tenth what does *I* mean?

To find what *who* stands for here we must get an answer to our question.

The word I should always be a Capital.

To the Teacher.—The pronoun, which has before been mentioned incidentally, is here treated more specially, but still informally.

The helping words in these sentences may be brought out by questions, especially the words *neatly, now,* and *soon.* Let the pupils find different positions for these words.

Joining Sentences.

Pupils will see that the sentences in the "exercises" may be combined into a talk about gardening.

In putting the sentences together, guard the pupils against using too many *ands* or other connectives, and against putting together sentences that are better separate.

LESSON XXVII.

Statements Changed to Questions — Chief Parts.

Copy the following sentences:—

John has spaded the garden.
Has John spaded the garden?
He is making the beds.
Is he making the beds?

What to See and Do.—How does the first question differ from the first statement?

How does the second question differ from the second statement?

Turn to the sentences in Lesson XXVI., and beginning with the third, change each statement except the tenth to a question.

Tell how this is done.

Now you may make a question of the tenth sentence, but in doing so you must be sure to change *will* to *shall*.

Say *Shall I?* not *Will I?*

Notice that the eleventh is already a question.

Was this made a question by changing the places of the chief words?

EXERCISE.

1. To-day I will plant potatoes.
2. To-morrow I will sow radish seed.
3. On Tuesday I will weed the lettuce.
4. On Wednesday I will hoe the cabbages.

What to Do and See.—Change each of these statements to a question.

Remember that in a question *will* is not used with *I.*
Remember that *I* must be a capital.
What do you here learn about the hyphen?
Find the chief parts in each sentence.
What does *to-day* tell?
What does the phrase *on Wednesday* tell?
What does *potatoes* tell?
In writing these sentences be careful of your spelling.

Additional Work.

To the Teacher.—Let the pupils become familiar with the form of a question made by putting the first word of the compound verb before the subject.

For additional work the sentences in Lesson XXII. and XXIV. may be changed to questions. Pupils will see that *saw, sprang,* and *licked* change to *did see, did spring,* and *did lick.*

Possibly the pupils may be led to see that in "I *will*" the speaker promises or says that he is willing, and that in "I *shall*" he simply tells what he is going to do.

They will see that a person does not want to ask others whether he himself is willing. At least, they can learn that we do not use "*Will I?*" and "*Will we?*"

LESSON XXVIII.

Different Kinds of Sentences.

Name of the One Addressed—Comma.

To the Teacher.—This cut will suggest oral work and sentence writing.

Copy the sentences below :—

Helen, here is a pretty flower.
Willie, do flowers have legs?
O Helen, how much this butterfly looks like a flower!
Thomas, put the net over him.

What to See.—What two kinds of sentences end with a period?

Read the statement found in the preceding lines.

Read the command.

Tell what each of the other sentences is.

In the first sentence, *is* is the chief word that tells.

What does it tell about?

You see that the verb sometimes comes before the subject.

What word tells what kind of flower?

What word tells where the flower is?

You see that the word *Helen* does not help either chief word.

Willie here uses Helen's name just to call her attention before making his statement.

So we separate the name *Helen* from the statement by a comma.

In the second sentence, is the question complete without the name of the one spoken to?

When we address a person with some feeling or excitement, we often put *O* before the name.

Is the third sentence complete without *O Helen?*

The word O should always be a Capital.

Read the command without the name of the one addressed.

Does it make complete sense?

Notice that in each of these four different kinds of sentences *the name of the one addressed is separated from the rest of the sentence by the* Comma.

Additional Work.

To the Teacher.—Encourage the pupils to talk about the butterfly or some other subject and to make different kinds of sentences introduced by the name of the one addressed.

Some of these should be written.

Dictation.

The script sentences may be written from dictation.

LESSON XXIX.

Different Kinds of Sentences.

Name of the One Addressed—Comma.

Copy the following sentences:—

Here, Helen, is a pretty flower.
Here is a pretty flower, Helen.
Do flowers have legs, Willie?

What to See.—What differences can you find between the first sentence above and the first in Lesson XXVIII.?

Look for position, capitals, and commas.

How does the second sentence above differ from the two just compared?

How does the third above compare with the second in Lesson XXVIII.?

When is a comma put after the name of the one spoken to?

When is it put before?
When is one comma put before and another after?

Copy these two sentences:—

> *Look at the spots, Edith, on his wings.*
>
> *See the little knobs, Harry, on his feelers.*

What to See.—How many commas are needed to separate *Edith* from the rest of the sentence?

How many to separate *Harry?* Why?

In each of these sentences find two other places for the name of the one addressed.

Where should the comma be put when these changes are made?

When *Edith* and *Harry* are put at the beginning, what capitals are changed to small letters? Why?

In the sentence—

"*Harry, see the knobs,*"

see is the word that tells some one to do something, but *Harry* is not the subject.

The word *Harry* simply calls attention, then the command follows.

In these commands the subject is left out.

We say that the subject *you* is "understood."

In all the commands you have written, *you*, "understood," has been the subject.

Additional Work.

To the Teacher.—For another lesson, different kinds of sentences containing the name of the one addressed may be found by the aid of the pupils, and put on the board.

Let the pupils write these, making the changes suggested here, when the sense will admit.

LESSON XXX.

Making and Joining Sentences.

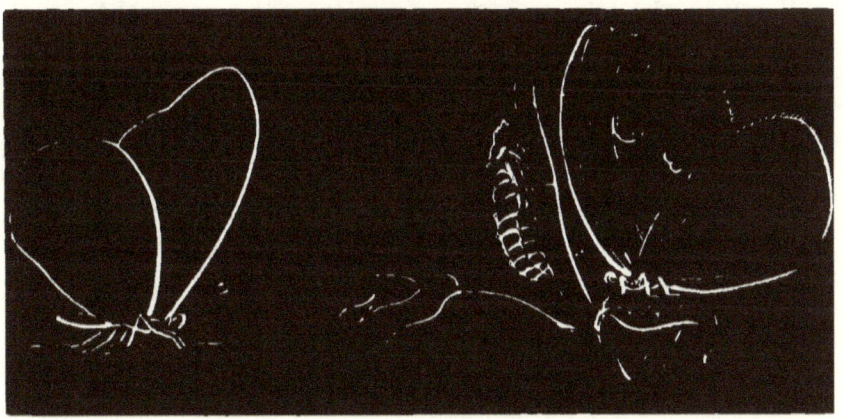

Oral Composition—The Butterfly.

To the Teacher.—This cut and the preceding one will aid the pupils in talking about the form and the parts of the butterfly. If specimens can be obtained, the interest will be greatly increased.

The pupils may be led to tell what they have themselves observed or learned in any way.

With some aid from the teacher—perhaps two or three head-lines on the board—the oral composition work may be put in order.

HINTS FOR WRITTEN COMPOSITION.

Butterfly, insect—body in three parts—six legs, middle part, under side—four wings, middle part, upper side—two feelers, little knobs—rests, holds wings up together—what you have seen—what you think about it.

What to Do.—Get what help you can from the hints above and make a short composition.

Try to make your sentences read together smoothly.

What to See.—Notice that in Lessons XXVIII. and XXIX. we use *him* and *his* in place of *butterfly*.

Here we use *it*.

We may use *he, his,* and *him;* we may use *she* and *her;* we may use *it* and *its;* but in making one sentence or one group of sentences, we must not change from one of these sets of words to another.

A GATHERING UP.

To the Teacher.—See "To the Teacher," p. 36.

A sentence has two **Chief Parts**—*the* **Subject** *and its* **Verb.**

The name of the thing we tell about is called the **Subject.**

The chief word that tells is called the **Verb.**

Particular Names *begin with capitals.*

The word **I** *should always be a capital.*

The word **O** *should always be a capital.*

Some **particular names** are made of **two or more words,** each of which begins with a capital.

Some **verbs** are made of **two or more words.**

The words **I, you, he, she, it, they, who, which,** etc., are used to **take the place of names.**

The name of the one addressed is separated from the rest of the sentence by a **Comma** *or by two commas.*

In telling a story we use helping words where they will make our word picture clear and strong.

We make our sentences read together smoothly.

We are careful not to use too many *ands,* and not to connect sentences that should be separate.

We make our reader anxious to know how the story is "coming out," and keep some of the most interesting things for the end.

Things Noticed in Passing.

We say "*Shall* I?" not "*Will* I?" (See Lesson XXVII.)

We may use *he, his,* and *him;* or *she* and *her;* or *it* and *its,* in speaking of an animal; but we must not change from one of these sets of words to another in the same sentence or the same group of sentences. (See Lesson XXX)

LESSON XXXI.

Writing Names—Abbreviations.

Christian and Family Names.

Copy these names:—

Ebenezer Webster.
Abigail Webster.
Daniel Webster.

What to See.—These names belong to a father, a mother, and their son.

Which word in each of these names shall we call the *family name?*

The first word in each of these names is called the *given name.*

It was *given* by the parents or some friend.

The **family name** is also called the **surname**.

The **given name** is also called the **Christian name**.

ORAL EXERCISES.

Name several great men, using only the *family* name.

Name some of your companions, using only the *given* name.

Would it seem respectful to speak of the ladies and gentlemen of your acquaintance by the *surname* alone?

WRITING NAMES—ABBREVIATIONS.

Do you think they would like you to use only their *Christian* names?

Give the surnames of several married ladies and pronounce the word *missis* before each.

Give the surnames of several unmarried ladies or girls with *miss* before each.

Give the surnames of several gentlemen and use the word *mister* before each.

Give the full names of several boys and put the word *master* before each.

Copy these names:—

William Dean Howells.
Wm. Dean Howells.
Wm. D. Howells.
W. D. Howells.
Charles Dudley Warner.
Chas. Dudley Warner.
Chas. D. Warner.
C. D. Warner.

What to See.—Here are four ways of writing the name of each of these men.

How should each word in a particular name begin?
Which are the surnames?
Which are the Christian names?
In the second form of writing Mr. Howells's name, how is *William* shortened?
How is the name shortened in the other forms?
How is Mr. Warner's name written?
When we write a name by itself, we put a period after it.
What other periods do you here discover?
These shortened forms are called **abbreviations**.
The first letter of a word is also called an **initial**.
A **Period** *is placed after an abbreviation or initial.*

LESSON XXXII.

Writing Names — Abbreviations — Titles.

Mr., Mrs., Miss.

Copy these names:—

Mister Francis Bret Harte.
Mr. F. Bret Harte.
Mistress Julia Ward Howe.
Mrs. Julia Ward Howe.
Miss Mary N. Murfree.

WRITING NAMES—ABBREVIATIONS—TITLES.

What to See.—How is the title *Mister* shortened?

The full form of *mister* is seldom written.

How is the title *Mistress* shortened?

This word, when put before a name as a title of respect, is not written in full, and in speaking it is shortened into *missis*.

Miss, the title of an unmarried lady or a young girl, is not shortened.

How many abbreviations do you find here?

Which of these are initials?

What do you find after each abbreviation or initial?

Do you find a period after *Miss?* Why?

EXERCISES FOR WRITING.

Write your own name in two or more ways.

Write the name of some girl and put the title *Miss* before it.

Write the name of some boy and put the title *Master* before it. (Do not shorten *Master*.)

Write the name of some gentleman and the name of some married lady, using the proper titles and abbreviations.

Write some of these names in more ways than one.

To the Teacher.—In continuing these exercises, attention may be called to such forms as *Mr. F. Bret Harte* for *Mr. Francis Bret Harte*, and *John G. Whittier* for *John Greenleaf Whittier*, in which either of the two Christian names may be written in full, as preferred by the owner.

At present social usage does not favor the abbreviation of Christian names.

LESSON XXXIII.

Writing Names — Abbreviations — Titles.

Rev., Prof., Dr.

Copy the names below: —

Rev. John Henry Newman.
Rev. J. H. Newman.
Professor Moses Coit Tyler.
Prof. M. C. Tyler.
Doctor Silas Weir Mitchell.
Dr. S. Weir Mitchell.

What to See.—*Reverend* is a title given to clergymen.
How is this title shortened?
Professor is a title given to some teachers.
How is this title shortened?
How is the title *Doctor* shortened?
What other abbreviations do you find here?
Which of these are initials?
What mark after each?
In each of these names tell the surname, the Christian names, and the title.

EXERCISES FOR WRITING.

Write the name of some clergyman whom you know.
Write the name of some doctor whom you know.
Write the name of some professor.
With each of these use the proper title abbreviated.

To the Teacher.—Names of well-known persons may be dictated or given to copy, till the pupils are familiar with all the titles and abbreviations that have been given.

The spelling of proper names—especially Christian names—deserves attention.

LESSON XXXIV.

Names — Addresses.

EXERCISE.

The Reverend Edward Everett Hale
lives in Boston.
Boston is in Massachusetts.

Copy this line:—

Rev. E. E. Hale, Boston, Mass.

What to See.—Notice that this group of words is made by shortening and putting together the two sentences at the beginning of the lesson.

Notice two commas in this group.

What words are left out where the first comma is found?

What words are left out where the second comma is found?

Tell how each abbreviation in this group is made.

The name of a person, with the name of the place where he lives or does business, is called his **Address.**

Copy these addresses :—

    Mr. Maurice Thompson,
        Crawfordsville,
            Montgomery Co.,
                Ind.

    Mr. Thomas Bailey Aldrich,
        4 Park St.,
            Boston,
                Mass.

What to See.—Notice that each of these two addresses is made up of four parts, put in four lines.

The second line of each address begins farther to the right than the first line, and the third farther than the second, and the fourth farther than the third.

These addresses are arranged as they should be on a letter envelope.

In giving the residence of Mr. Thompson, we give his **post-office, county,** and **state.**

In the next address we put the **number of the house** and the **name of the street** together, and then give the **city** and the **state.**

Where do you find commas in these addresses?

What do you find at the end of each address?

Notice that the period after *Mass.* answers for the abbreviation and also for the end of the address.

Find two new abbreviations in these addresses.

They are for *county* and *street*.

Dictation.

To the Teacher.—The three addresses here given may be dictated in the shortened form, or they may be put on the board in sentence form for pupils to shorten and arrange.

LESSON XXXV.

Names — Addresses.

EXERCISE.

Miss Lucy Field lives at Orlando. Orlando is in Orange County. Orange County is in Florida.

Master Tommy Dodd lives at 10 Euclid Avenue. Euclid Avenue is in Cleveland. Cleveland is in Ohio.

Copy these two addresses :—

Miss Lucy Field,
  Orlando,
    Orange Co.,
      Fla.

Master Tommy Dodd,
  10 Euclid Av.,
    Cleveland,
      Ohio.

What to See.—How many parts in each of these addresses?

What mark follows each part?

What do you discover as to the place of beginning the lines in each address?

This is the way to write an address on a letter envelope.

Compare each shortened form with the longer form of the same address, and notice what words are left out and how the sentences are put together.

Tell how each abbreviation is made.

Av. is an abbreviation of what?

What two uses has the period after *Fla.*?
What use has the period after *Ohio*?
Notice that there is **no period after** *Miss or Master*.
Are these words abbreviations?
Notice that in the first line of this lesson we say "*at* Orlando," and in the second line of Lesson XXXIV. we say "*in* Boston."

We say "lives *at* ——" if the place is small, or it seems to us distant and not very important.

We say "lives *in* ——" if the place is a large city or some division of the country.

In the fourth line of this lesson we say "lives *at* 10 Euclid Av."

If we do not give the house number, we say "lives *in* —— Street."

EXERCISES FOR WRITING.

Write your own address. If you live in a city, use the second model; if not, use the first.

Write the address of some friend in the country.

Write the address of some friend in the city.

Dictation.

To the Teacher.—The addresses here given and others should be written from dictation.

One or two additional lessons may be profitable, as affording exercises in spelling, capitals, and abbreviations, as well as in the form of addresses.

The use of the prepositions *at* and *in*, as noted above, may be further emphasized. Lasting impressions are often best made by calling attention to such things incidentally, as they naturally present themselves.

Such forms as the following may at first be put on the board to aid the pupil :—

  Name,   Name,
   Post-office,   House Number and Street,
    County,   City,
     State.   State.

LESSON XXXVI.

Names — Days, Months, and Seasons.

Copy the names below :—

Sunday, Monday, Tuesday, Wednesday, Thursday, Friday, Saturday.

January, February, March, April, May, June, July, August, September, October, November, December, spring, summer, autumn, winter.

What to See.—The name of each day of the week begins with what kind of letter?

The name of each day of the month begins with what kind of letter?

With what kind of letter does the name of each season begin?

What mark separates the names in each group?

What mark at the end of each group?

Learn to spell each name.

LESSON XXXVII.

Abbreviations—Days and Months.

Copy the abbreviations below :—

Sun., Mon., Tues., Wed., Thurs., Fri., Sat.

Jan., Feb., Mar., Apr., Aug., Sep., Oct., Nov., Dec.

What to See.—Tell how each abbreviation in the first group is made.

Tell how each abbreviation in the second group is made.

What names of the months are not here abbreviated?

It is better not to abbreviate these short names.

What mark after each abbreviation?

What mark separates the abbreviations of each group?

Learn to make these abbreviations from memory.

To the Teacher.—Let the pupils learn the names of the days and months in order, and then let them write the abbreviations in order, without the aid of the book, inserting the names not abbreviated, to prevent confusion.

LESSON XXXVIII.

Names — Dates.

EXERCISE.

Columbus first saw the New World on the 12*th day of October in the year* 1492.

The Declaration of Independence was signed on the 4*th day of July in the year* 1776.

Washington was born on the 22d *day of February in the year* 1732.

Copy the dates below:—

Oct. 12, 1492.

July 4, 1776.

Feb. 22, 1732.

What to See.—Notice that the first date copied is a shorter form of the date in the first sentence.

Tell what changes are made to get this shorter form.

Do the same for each of the other dates.

Notice that the month and the day of the month are put together, and that the comma separates them from the year.

The first date in script should be read *October twelfth, fourteen hundred and ninety-two.*

Read the other two dates.

Copy these dates:—

May 1st, June 2d, Aug. 3d, Sep. 4th, Oct. 5th, Nov. 6th.

What to See.—You find no period after *1st, 2d, 3d, 4th,* and the like, as you do after abbreviations.

The period after *6th* is only to mark the end of the whole group.

1st, 2d, 4th are read *first, second, fourth.*

The day of the month is often written as above.

Write the date of your birth.

Write other dates that you remember.

LESSON XXXIX.

Names — Letters.

Copy the following letter carefully, and try to see everything in it:—

Liberty, Casey Co., Ky.,
Aug. 21, 1891.

Dear Jennie,

On Tuesday my cousin Bertha and I are going to visit Uncle Joshua and Aunt Rachel at Clover Top. We take the Olive Branch R. R. to Fox Hollow, where cousin Reuben Rice will meet us with his ponies, Dexter and Lightfoot.

Your friend,
Emma Hill.

What to See.—The first line at the right tells where Emma Hill is when she writes.

How are the post-office, the county, and the state separated?

The next line tells when Emma writes—it gives the *date* of the letter.

What separates the **place** from the **date**?

What three things are given in this date?

What does the comma in the date separate?

What mark after the date?

Emma now wants to greet her friend pleasantly, so she writes *Dear Jennie* on a separate line.

In the next line she goes on to tell Jennie the news.

At the end of the letter Emma again wants to show her friendship, so she puts *Your friend* on a line by itself, and then signs her own name below.

Notice that Emma writes *Uncle* and *Aunt* with capitals, making each a part of a particular name.

You see that she does not think of *cousin* as a part of Reuben Rice's name.

You find in this letter the new abbreviations **Ky., R. R.**

They are for *Kentucky* and *Railroad*.

After *Dear Jennie* notice the capital **O** in *on*.

This is the custom in writing letters.

Notice that Emma says **Bertha and I,** putting herself last. This is polite.

Notice that *Your friend* begins with a capital.

You can explain all the other capitals.

Notice that Emma, in writing her news, puts her lines into two groups. These groups we call **Paragraphs.**

Mark out an envelope on your slate, and put on the address as here :—

```
                                    ┌───────┐
                                    │ STAMP │
                                    └───────┘


            Miss Jennie Dale,
               Bethel,
                    Giles Co.,
                         Tenn.
```

What to See.—Tell all you can about this address.

Remember that you learned about addresses in Lessons XXXIV. and XXXV.

Tenn. is the abbreviation for *Tennessee.*

Where is the postage stamp placed?

LESSON XL.

Names — Letters.

Copy the following letter carefully, and try to see everything in it :—

20 Sake St., Buffalo, N. Y.,
June 20, 1892.

Dear Mamma,

Papa and I had a jolly time Saturday at Niagara Falls.

After tramping through Goat Island and Luna Island, we went across the Suspension Bridge to Canada. But, O mamma! I cannot write one half of what I saw.

Your affectionate son,

Dick.

***What to See.*—**Where was this letter written? (*New York* is here abbreviated **N. Y.**)

When was it written?

What two words are used for a loving salute?

Where does the first word of the main part, or *body,* of the letter begin?

At the end, what words show Dick's loving regard for his mother?

Read the *place* and the *date* together.

What four things are given in the place?

Which two are put together?

Into how many parts do the commas divide the place?

What three things are given in the date?

Which two are put together?

What are separated by the comma?

What separates the *place* from the *date?*

Notice the comma after *Dear Mamma,* and the one after *Your affectionate son.*

Notice that Dick says ***Papa and I,*** not *I and papa.*

In *Dear Mamma, mamma* begins with a capital, although it is a common name.

Any name, common or particular, used as this is, begins with a capital.

Notice *O mamma!* farther down.

From what you learned in Lessons XXVIII. and XXIX. about the name of the one addressed, you might look for a comma after *mamma* as well as one before *O ;* but Dick puts an exclamation mark in place of the second comma, to show his feeling.

How many paragraphs has Dick made of the body of his letter?

How does he show where one paragraph ends and another begins?

Tell what you can about the capitals and the periods.

Mark out an envelope on your slate, and put on the address as here:—

> Mrs. Richard Ross,
> 150 State St.,
> Chicago,
> Ill.
>
> STAMP

What to See.—Try to remember what you learned in Lessons XXXIV., XXXV., and XXXIX. about addresses, and then tell all you can about this.

Ill. is the abbreviation for *Illinois*.

Tell on what part of the envelope the different lines are written.

On what corner is the postage stamp?

Additional Lessons.

To the Teacher.—We prefer not to confuse the pupils with a variety of letter forms here. Let them first become thoroughly acquainted with the simplest form.

We do not think it well to use here the terms *Heading, Salutation, Complimentary Address*, etc.

Dictation.

These letters may be dictated, and then compared with the book for correction.

Original Letters.

Each pupil should write a "real letter."

In such, the pupil may use his own name and place, and give the true date of writing.

This letter may be corrected, rewritten, and sent by mail, or put into the "school post-office."

Such letters should be short, that they may be very carefully done.

It may be well to limit the pupils to some subject, requiring them, for instance, to tell what happened, or what they did, on some day of particular importance to them.

Reviews.

The letters here given for copying are made to serve as reviews.

The work suggested in our observation exercises may be emphasized and continued.

A GATHERING UP.

To the Teacher.—See "To the Teacher," p. 36.

A person's name is made up of a *family name*, or surname, and one or more *given names*, or **Christian names**.

Shortened words are called Abbreviations.
The first letter of a name is called an Initial.
A **Period** *is placed after an abbreviation or initial.*

Abbreviations.

Mr., Mister.
Mrs., Mistress.
Dr., Doctor.
Prof., Professor.
Rev., Reverend.
St., Street.
Av., Avenue.
Co., County.
Chas., Charles.
Wm., William.
Geo., George.
Fla., Florida.
Tenn., Tennessee.
N. Y., New York.
Mass., Massachusetts.
Ky., Kentucky.
Ill., Illinois.

R. R., Railroad.
Sun., Sunday.
Mon., Monday.
Tues., Tuesday.
Wed., Wednesday.
Thurs., Thursday.
Fri., Friday.
Sat., Saturday.
Jan., January.
Feb., February.
Mar., March.
Apr., April.
Aug., August.
Sep., September.
Oct., October.
Nov., November.
Dec., December.

The name of a person, with the name of the place where he lives or does business, is called his **Address.**

For the residence of a person in the country, give the **post-office,** the **county,** and the **state.**

For the residence of a person in the city, give the **number of the house,** the **name of the street,** the **city,** and the **state.**

The names of the days of the week and the months of the year begin with **Capitals,** *but the names of the seasons begin with small letters.*

In writing a **date,** put the **month** and the **day** together, and separate them from the **year** by a comma.

In a **letter,** give the **place** and the **date** of writing, a **friendly or courteous greeting,** and then write the main part, or **body.** After this write a **friendly or courteous closing** line, and sign your **name.**

(For the form and position of these parts, see Lessons XXXIX. and XL.)

Things Noticed in Passing.

We say "lives at ——," if the place is small.

We say "lives in ——," if the place is a large city, or a division of the country.

We say "lives at 10 Grand Street," etc.

We say "lives in" a certain street. (See Lesson XXXV.)

We say "**Bertha and I,**" "**papa and I,**" etc.; not "I and Bertha," etc. (See Lessons XXXIX. and XL.)

LESSON XLI.

Chief Names and Their Verbs — Adding *S*.

EXERCISE.

1. The frog croak*s*.
2. The frog*s* croak.
3. The swallow twitter*s*.
4. The swallow*s* twitter.
5. The lamb bleat*s*.
6. The lamb*s* bleat.
7. The rooster crow*s*.
8. The rooster*s* crow.
9. The brook babble*s*.
10. The brook*s* babble.

What to See and Do.—What differences can you find between the first and the second sentence?

The word *frogs* means more than one—it may be two or hundreds.

Would it sound right to say, *Frogs croaks?*

Find the differences between the sentences in each of the other groups.

When the verb tells what one thing does, how does it end?

How can a name be made to mean more than one?

Write five sentences each telling what one thing does, and then change them to tell what two or more things do.

LESSON XLII.

Chief Names and Their Verbs—Adding S.

EXERCISE.

1. The wind blow*s*.
2. The wind*s* blow.

3. The bough bend*s*.
4. The bough*s* bend.

5. The bud swell*s*.
6. The bud*s* swell.

7. The squirrel leap*s*.
8. The squirrel*s* leap.

What to See and Do.—Find the differences between the first and the second sentence above.

Do the same for each of the other three pairs of sentences.

Notice that these verbs ending in *s* all tell what one thing *does*, not what it *did* in the past or *will do* in some time to come.

The wind blew.
The wind*s* blew.
The wind will blow.
The wind*s* will blow.

Look at these four sentences, and see whether the verb adds *s* when it tells what one thing *did* or *will do*.

When a verb tells what one thing does, how does it end?

How can a name be made to mean more than one?

Write five sentences each telling what one thing does, and then change them to tell what two or more things do.

To the Teacher.—The words *bough* and *blew* in these sentences suggest exercises on the homonyms:—

>   bough,   blew,
>   bow;   blue.

LESSON XLIII.

Chief Names and Their Verbs—*Is* and *Are*.

EXERCISE.

1. The wind *is* blowing.
2. The wind*s* *are* blowing.

3. The bough *is* bending.
4. The bough*s* *are* bending.

5. The bud *is* swelling.
6. The bud*s* *are* swelling.

7. The squirrel *is* leaping.
8. The squirrel*s* *are* leaping.

What to See.—What differences do you find between the first sentence and the second?

Examine each of the other three pairs of sentences, and tell what you discover.

When you use *is*, do you speak of one, or more than one?

When do you use *are?*

QUESTIONS.

Is the wind blowing?
Are the winds blowing?

What to See.—Point out the differences between these two sentences and the first two at the beginning of the lesson.

How may each of the other six sentences be changed to a question?

EXCLAMATIONS.

How the wind *is* blowing!
How the winds *are* blowing!

What to See.—Find the differences between these two sentences and the two at the beginning of the lesson.

Is is used in speaking of what?

Are is used in speaking of what?

EXERCISES FOR WRITING.

Write statements using *is* and *are*.
Write questions using *is* and *are*.
Write exclamations using *is* and *are*.
Change your statements to questions.

LESSON XLIV.

Chief Names and Their Verbs—*Was* and *Were.*

EXERCISE.

1. The wind *was* blowing.
2. The wind*s were* blowing.

3. The bough *was* bending.
4. The bough*s were* bending.

5. The bud *was* swelling.
6. The bud*s were* swelling.

7. The squirrel *was* leaping.
8. The squirrel*s were* leaping.

What to See.—Find the differences between the first and the second sentence of each group above.

Is *was* used in speaking of one thing, or more than one thing?

Is *were* used in speaking of one thing, or more than one thing?

QUESTIONS.

Was the wind blowing?
Were the winds blowing?

What to See.—What differences can you find between these two sentences and the two at the beginning of this lesson?

How may each of the other sentences be changed to a question?

EXCLAMATIONS.

How the wind *was* blowing!
How the winds *were* blowing!

What to See and Do.—How do these two sentences differ from the first two at the beginning of this lesson?

Write a statement, a question, and an exclamation, using *was,* and then change each so as to use *were*.

LESSON XLV.

A Study of Sentences — Putting Sentences Together.

EXERCISE.

1. A faint gray light begins to steal over the woods.
2. A faint gray light begins to steal over the fields.
3. The stars all fade out from the sky.
4. They fade out one by one.
5. A light breeze springs up.
6. The breeze sets the leaves and the flowers all nodding and whispering to each other.

What to See.—In each of these sentences we have underlined the verb.

You may find the subject.

Which of the subjects mean but one ?
How do their verbs end ?
Which subjects mean more than one ?
Do their verbs add *s ?*

Copy the following :—

WATCHING THE SUN RISE.

A faint gray light begins to steal over the woods and the fields. The stars all fade out one by one from the sky, and a light breeze springs up, which sets the leaves and the flowers all nodding and whispering to each other.

What to See.—Which of the sentences given at the beginning of the lesson are here put together ?

Can you tell how it is done ?

You have learned that *which* can take the place of a name and help to join sentences.

It can also take the place of *breeze*. Try *it* in place of *breeze* in the last sentence, and see whether it will join the sentences as *which* does.

To the Teacher.—The pupils may change the verbs in these sentences to *began, faded, sprang,* and *set,* and so describe the sunrise as past.

Let them see that no *s* is now added.

Help them to see the beauty of the selection above. Let them see how it helps the picture to imagine the leaves and flowers to be like persons.

Let them note the commas between the sentences connected by *and* and *which.* Easy questions may bring out some of the helping words.

LESSON XLVI.

A Study of Sentences — Using the Chief Parts Correctly.

EXERCISE.

1. The little birds begin to twitter.
2. They call softly to their friends.
3. Their friends are in the branches above and below.
4. The sun is coming.
5. The sun makes them happy.
6. Perhaps they are telling each other this.
7. The light grows stronger and stronger.
8. Very soon the sun shows its bright rim above the hills.
9. It flings its golden beams over the trees and the houses.

What to See and Do.—In each of these nine sentences we have underlined the verb.

You may find the subject.

Which of these verbs tell about one thing?

Which tell about more than one?

Which of these subjects are made to mean more than one by adding *s*?

Use *was* or *were* in each of the sentences above, thus: "The little birds *were* beginning to twitter."

Make the nine sentences above read together smoothly.

LESSON XLVII.

Putting Sentences Together.

Copy the following:—

WATCHING THE SUN RISE—*Continued.*

The little birds begin to twitter and call softly to their friends in the branches above and below. Perhaps they are telling each other that the sun is coming to make them happy.

The light grows stronger and stronger. Very soon the sun shows its bright rim above the hills, and flings its golden beams over the trees and the houses.

What to See and Do.—Notice how the first three sentences of Lesson XLVI. have here been put into one.

In this new sentence *birds* and *begin* are the chief words, and all the others are now helpers.

How many sentences of Lesson XLVI. are put into the next sentence?

What has been done with the last three sentences of Lesson XLVI.?

Why were the sentences above put into two paragraphs?

Describe the sunrise as past, and find other ways of putting the sentences together.

To the Teacher.—The word *sun* above suggests exercises on the homonyms:—

sun, son.

LESSON XLVIII.

Composition — Hints.

When you went to see the sun rise, how did you get started? Where did you go?

Did the sun come up from behind a hill?

In what direction did you look?

After the sun was up, did the birds burst into loud song? What voice was first and loudest? What voices joined in? What happened then? What did the flowers do? What did the insects do?

Do you think it a pity that people are not up, like the birds, at daybreak? Why?

What to Do.—Get what help you can from these " hints " and make a short composition.

LESSON XLIX.

Have and *Has, Do* and *Does.*

EXERCISE.

1. The wind *has* blown.
2. The winds *have* blown.
3. The bough *has* bent.
4. The boughs *have* bent.
5. The bud *has* swollen.
6. The buds *have* swollen.

What to See and Do.—Compare the two sentences in each of these three groups.

With what kind of names is *has* used ?

With what kind of names is *have* used ?

Change each sentence to a question, and tell how it is done.

EXERCISE.

1. The wind *does* blow.
2. The wind*s* *do* blow.

3. The bough *does* bend.
4. The bough*s* *do* bend.

5. The bud *does* swell.
6. The bud*s* *do* swell.

What to See and Do.—With what names is *does* used ?

With what names is *do* used ?

You notice that we say *does blow* and *do blow* when we wish to speak with emphasis.

Write a statement, a question, and an exclamation, using *does*, then change each so as to use *do*.

To the Teacher.—The illustrations that we have given of the use of *-s*, *is*, *are*, *was*, *were*, *have*, *has*, *do*, *does*, may be sufficient to show how the verb agrees with its subject. Full formal rules or statements are not here desired.

There is danger of spending too much time in multiplying these short, unrelated sentences, in which there is little, if any, liability to error.

LESSON L.
Using Verbs with *I* and *You*.

What to See and Do.—Use *I* for subject, where you can, in the sentences of Lesson XLI.

Do the verbs add *s* with *I?*

Use *you* in the same sentences where you can.

Do verbs add *s* with *you?*

Change the same sentences so as to use

is, are, was, were,
have, has, do, does,

and see which will take *I* for subject.

See how many of these verbs will take *you* for subject.

You found that *I* needed

am, was, have, do.

Write statements using *are, were, have,* and *do* with the subject *you.*

Change each of these statements to a question.

You may stand for **one or more than one,** but its **verb** is always used as if *you* meant **more than one;** as, "You *are;*" "You *were.*"

To the Teacher.—We suggest much oral practice on short sentences, using "You *were;*" "*Were* you?" etc. Such sentences as "I was there yesterday," "I was in time," may be put on the board. The pupils may change *I* to *you* and repeat the sentences rapidly, first as statements, then as questions.

LESSON LI.

The Contractions *Isn't, Aren't,* Etc.

Copy the following very carefully:—

*Isn't, wasn't, hasn't, doesn't,
aren't, weren't, haven't, don't.*

What to See and Do.—The first word of these script lines is made up of *is* and *not.*

Notice that a little mark is placed between *n* and *t* to show where the *o* is left out.

This mark is like a comma, but it is higher up.

Describe each of the other words.

Make four sentences, using the words of the first line in telling about one thing; as,

The drone doesn't work.

Make four sentences, using the words of the second line in telling about more than one thing; as,

The drones don't work.

Do work is the chief part that tells. The word *not* denies what the other words tell.

These forms at the beginning of the lesson are called **contractions.**

You see they have no period at the end as *abbreviations* have.

There is great danger of using **don't for doesn't.**
Use each of these words five times.

To the Teacher.—These exercises may be continued by changing the statements to questions.

Let such exercises be extended, and reviewed again and again till the tendency to say "He *don't*," etc., is overcome.

Test the pupils to find whether any are in the habit of using

ain't, hain't, 'tain't.

If such words are found in use, emphasize the fact that they are wrong, and give much oral drill.

LESSON LII.

Putting Sentences Together — Commas — Chief Names and Their Verbs.

EXERCISE.

1. On the bee's leg is a basket.
2. On the bee's leg is a brush.
3. On the bee's leg is a tool to press wax.

What to See.—Which generally comes first, the chief name, or the chief word that tells?

You see that in the first sentence we talk about a basket. What is the chief word that tells?

Read the phrase that helps by telling where the basket is.

In each of the other sentences pick out the chief parts, and then read the helping phrase that tells where.

Begin with the word *a* and read each sentence.

Copy the following :—

On the bee's leg are a basket, a brush, and a tool to press wax.

What to See.—You see that we have put our three subjects, *basket*, *brush*, and *tool*, together and said the same of all three things.

Now that we talk about three things, should we use *is*, or *are?*

Notice particularly that in putting together these three words we put *and* between the last two only, and then separate the three by commas.

In such sentences all the *ands* are sometimes put in, and then the commas are not needed.

EXERCISE.

1. A large cell is provided for the baby queen.
2. The best food is provided for the baby queen.
3. Delicate care is provided for the baby queen.

What to See and Do.—We have underlined the verb in each sentence.

Find the subject in each.

Are the chief parts here changed about as in the preceding " exercise " ?

Why do we use *is* in each sentence?

Begin with *for* and read each sentence.

Put the three sentences together as we did the three preceding.

Put them together again, and change the place of the helping phrase, *for the baby queen.*

LESSON LIII.

Putting Sentences Together — Commas — Chief Names and Their Verbs.

EXERCISE.

1. The fly has six legs.
2. The bee has six legs.
3. The wasp has six legs.
4. The ant has six legs.
5. Other insects have six legs.

What to See.—Find the two chief parts in each sentence.

Why is *has* used in the first four?

Why is *have* used in the last?

Copy the following :—

The fly, the bee, the wasp, the ant, and other insects have six legs.

What to See.—We have here put together five subjects and then said the same of all the things.

How many commas are used to separate the subjects?
Where is the *and* placed?

EXERCISE.

1. Moths steal the bees' honey.
2. Snails steal the bees' honey.
3. Wasps steal the bees' honey.
4. Other foes steal the bees' honey.

What to See and Do.—Change *moths* to mean but one, then read the sentence.

What other changes do you find?
Change the other subjects in the same way.
When do you find *s* added to the verb?
When do you find *s* added to the subject?
Join these four sentences as the five preceding sentences were joined.
How many commas have you used with the four subjects that you have joined?
Where did you put the word that connects?

To the Teacher.—Let the pupils make and put together sentences of their own.

The use of the apostrophe in the word *bees'*, found above, may be explained as showing that the bees own, or possess, the honey. Let the pupils see that the *s* here means more than one bee. Let them compare this possessive with the one in Lesson LII.

LESSON LIV.

Putting Sentences Together — Commas — Chief Names and Their Verbs.

EXERCISE.

1. A fly does not grow after getting legs and wings.
2. A bee does not grow after getting legs and wings.
3. A wasp does not grow after getting legs and wings.

What to See and Do.—We have marked the verbs.

Notice that each verb is made up of two words.

What does the little word between the two parts of the verb do?

Make contractions in these sentences as we did in Lesson LI.

Should you here use *doesn't*, or *don't?*

Begin with *after* and read each of the three sentences above.

Read each, and put the helping phrase, *after getting legs and wings*, between the subject and its verb.

Put the three sentences together.

Tell how it was done.

EXERCISE.

1. Spiders spin.
2. Spiders weave.
3. Spiders hunt.

Copy the following :—

Spiders spin, weave, and hunt.

What to See.—In the script we use the word *spider* but once, and then put the three verbs together as we put together the names in the other exercises.

Notice that we use the commas and the *and* as we did when we put names together.

EXERCISE.

1. The fly does not grow after getting legs.
2. The fly does not grow after getting wings.

Copy the following :—

The fly does not grow after getting legs and wings.

What to See.—Notice that we here put together the two words that differ, and use all the others but once.

You see that the parts joined may be chief parts or helpers.

Notice that when there are but two things connected and the connecting word is put in, no comma is needed.

Additional Work—Commas.

To the Teacher.—The change here suggested in the order of the phrases found in the first "exercise" may give occasion for illustrating the use of the comma to set off a word or phrase that breaks in between the parts of a sentence.

Pupils can easily be taught to see that commas aid the reader by showing where slight breaks are made in the sentence.

Few *rules* are needed.

LESSON LV.

A Study of Sentences — Putting Sentences Together.

EXERCISE.

1. Here is a fly.
2. This fly lives in our houses.
3. See his two large eyes.
4. They take up nearly the whole of his head.
5. The fly has two wings.
6. The butterfly has four wings.
7. The bee has four wings.
8. Most other insects have four wings.

What to See.—We have underlined the verbs. You may find the subjects.

Why is *is* used in the first sentence?
What word tells where the fly is?
Why is *s* needed with *lives*?
What little phrase tells where this fly lives?
Is the next sentence a statement?
The subject *you* is left out.
Why does *take* not end in *s*?
Tell why *has* and *have* are used correctly in these sentences.

Copy the following:—

WATCHING A FLY.

Here is the fly that lives in our houses.

See his two eyes that take up nearly the whole of his head.

The fly has two wings, but the butterfly, the bee, and most other insects have four wings.

What to See.—We make *that* take the place of *fly* in the second sentence of the "exercise," and so we join the first two sentences.

You will remember that *which* has done this same work for us.

Tell how we join the next two sentences.

Tell how the last three sentences of the "exercise" are put together.

Find in the new sentence the three subjects of *have*.
How are these subjects connected?
Where is *and* understood?
What have you learned about the commas here used?
What does the word *but* join?
Can you see why a comma is needed before *but,* and not before *that?*

Watching a Fly—*Continued.*

EXERCISE.

1. The fly has three pairs of legs.
2. With these he runs very nimbly.
3. He doesn't jump.
4. Watch him.
5. See him brush his head.
6. See him clean his head.
7. He uses his fore legs as hands.

What to See and Do.—How many statements here?
How many commands?
Now put together, without help, such of these sentences as should go together.
Make what changes you like.
Make as many groups, or paragraphs, as you think proper.

To the Teacher.—Since the pupils are required to use, in these exercises, *fore* and *pair*, a lesson may be given on the use and spelling of the homonyms—

four, fore;
pair, pear, pare.

LESSON LVI.

A Study of Sentences — Putting Sentences Together.

EXERCISE.

1. The fly first brushes one side.
2. He then brushes the other side.
3. Then he rubs his legs together.
4. This drives the dust out of the hairs.
5. After this he gives himself the finishing touches.

What to See.—You may find the subjects of the verbs we have marked.

Why does each verb end in *s?*

Notice that *es*, a syllable, is added to *brush*.

It would be very hard to sound *s* after *sh*. Try it.

Copy the following:—

Watching a Fly—*Continued.*

The fly first brushes one side, then the other. Then he rubs his legs together to drive the dust out of the hairs. After this he gives himself the finishing touches.

What to See.—What words were left out in putting the first two sentences of the "exercise" together?

These words are understood—we do not need to repeat them.

Notice the comma.

Which sentence was changed to a long helping phrase?

WATCHING A FLY—*Continued*.

EXERCISE.

1. The fly has no jaws or teeth to eat with.
2. He has a tiny tube.
3. He sucks up his food through this.
4. We suck water through a straw in the same way.
5. He lets a drop of water fall from this tube on a piece of sugar.
6. The sugar softens.
7. He sucks up the sweet liquid.
8. He brushes and cleans himself carefully after every meal.
9. He uses his hairy legs for brushes.

What to Do.—Put these sentences together so that they will read easily and smoothly.

A GATHERING UP.

To the Teacher.—See "To the Teacher," p. 36.

A single verb adds s *to tell what one thing* does.

Is, was, has, *and* does *are used with subjects that mean but one.*

Are, were, have, *and* do *are used with subjects that mean more than one.*

Verbs with *I* and *you* do not add **s**.

Am, was, have, and *do* are used with *I*.

You may mean **one or more than one,** but the **verb** is always used as if *you* meant **more than one.**

Some **words** are **contracted** by leaving out letters and putting the apostrophe in their place.

CONTRACTIONS.

Isn't, wasn't, hasn't, doesn't, aren't, weren't, haven't, don't.

Be careful not to use **don't** for **doesn't**. **Ain't, hain't,** *'tain't* are incorrect.

Three or more words or phrases connected and used in the same way are generally separated by **Commas.**

LESSON LVII.

Names Changed to Mean *More than One.*

EXERCISE.

flower	bird	lamb	squirrel
flower**s**	bird**s**	lamb**s**	squirrel**s**
dress	ax	watch	thrush
dress**es**	ax**es**	watch**es**	thrush**es**

What to Do.—Make good sentences, using all the names that end in s or es.

Change your sentences and make these names mean one thing.

Be sure to find whether other words need changing.

Learn to spell the words of the "exercise."

Names are made to mean more than one by adding s *or* es.

To the Teacher.—The exercise of changing sentences as suggested above is very valuable, and should be followed up.

LESSON LVIII.

Names Changed to Mean *More than One*.

EXERCISE.

| daisy | lily | poppy | pansy |
| dais*ies* | lil*ies* | popp*ies* | pans*ies* |

| valley | turkey | monkey | chimney |
| valley*s* | turkey*s* | monkey*s* | chimney*s* |

| wolf | leaf | proof | roof |
| wol*ves* | lea*ves* | proof*s* | roof*s* |

What to See and Do.—Notice that *some* of the *names* ending with y change the y to ie when s is added.

Some others, you see, do not change the *y*.

Notice that the latter have *e* before the *y*.

If a, e, or o is before the y, s is added without changing the y.

NAMES CHANGED TO MEAN MORE THAN ONE.

Tell how the other words are changed to mean more than one.

Learn to spell the words of the preceding "exercise."

EXERCISE.

1. The daisy, lily, poppy, and pansy are blooming in the valley.
2. The monkey has chased the turkey from the chimney.
3. The leaf falls on the roof.

What to See and Do.—Find five names in the first sentence.

Find the verb.

How many things does this verb tell about?

What have you learned about writing these names together?

Which name belongs to a helping phrase that tells where the flowers are blooming?

How many sentences can you make of the first sentence above?

Make them orally.

Of what is something said in the next sentence?

In this sentence two of the names are among the helping words.

One tells *what* the monkey has chased.

What does the other help to tell?

Find the chief parts of the third sentence.

What does the phrase *on the roof* tell?

Change these three sentences so as to make each name mean more than one.

LESSON LIX.

Names Changed to Show Possession.

Copy the following words carefully :—

daisy's lily's turkey's
pansy's wolf's monkey's

EXERCISE.

1. The *daisy's* petals fold at night.
2. The *lily's* cup shows beautiful tints.
3. The *pansy's* face peeps up.
4. The *turkey's* voice doesn't charm the ear.
5. Aren't that *monkey's* fingers in mischief?
6. The *wolf's* howl is ringing on the mountain.

What to See.—The apostrophe (') and s are joined to *daisy* to show that the daisy has, or possesses, petals.

The apostrophe and *s* are joined to *lily* to show that the lily has, or possesses, the cup.

Tell what the apostrophe and *s* show in each of the other sentences.

Notice that these names showing possession are all helping words joined to another name.

In the first sentence *petals* is the chief name.

We say the petals fold, not the daisy.

Daisy's tells whose petals fold, and so helps the subject.

Lily's tells whose cup.

Find what each of the other words showing possession does in the sentence.

Each of these names ending in *'s* means but one.

Notice that each simply adds *'s*, and that *y* is not changed to *ie*, nor *f* to *ve*, as in the preceding lesson.

Find in the "exercise" two contractions, and tell what the apostrophe stands for.

To the Teacher.—That each of these possessives means but one, and that the apostrophe precedes the *s*, should be impressed.

In the fourth and fifth sentences the pupil is liable to use the wrong verb. Exercises in repeating and changing these and similar sentences will be profitable.

Chief Parts and their Helpers.

The pupils should be able to point out the chief words and their helpers.

LESSON LX.

Names Changed to Show Possession — One and More than One.

Copy the following words carefully, and compare them with the words at the beginning of Lesson LIX.:—

daisies'   lilies'   turkeys'
pansies'   wolves'   monkeys'

EXERCISE.

1. The *daisies'* heads are nodding to us.
2. The *lilies'* cups are robbed by the bees.
3. The *pansies'* faces look like laughing fairies.
4. The *turkeys'* voices have suddenly stopped.
5. *Monkeys'* faces are grinning at us.
6. The *wolves'* voices answer each other.

What to See.—The apostrophe (') is joined to *daisies* to show that the daisies own, or possess, the heads.

You have learned that the *s* at the end of *daisies* makes the word mean more than one.

Here the apostrophe *alone* shows the possession.

The apostrophe is joined to *lilies* to show that the lilies own, or possess, the cups.

Tell what each of the other apostrophes shows.

Notice that these names showing possession are all helping words joined to another name.

Daisies' helps to picture the thing we are talking about by telling whose heads are nodding.

Lilies' helps the next subject by telling whose cups.

You may tell what each of the other words in italics does.

How many of the helping names above mean more than one?

How do you know?

To the Teacher.—That the *s* in these possessives is added to make the name mean more than one, and that the apostrophe is afterward added to show the possession, should be thoroughly understood.

Chief Parts and their Helpers.

We advise exercises in pointing out the chief words and noting their agreement, and in changing the number of the subjects that other necessary changes may be noted.

What the helping words do should be told, in a general way, by the pupils.

LESSON LXI.

How to Show Possession — One and More than One.

Copy the following carefully :—

baby's nose	wren's song
babies' noses	wrens' songs
calf's food	Maggie's hat
calves' food	lady's dress
Harry's kite	ladies' dresses
America's flag	George's drum.

What to See.—Are any of these expressions sentences? Why?

Which of the names copied are common names?

Which are particular names?

What have you learned about such names?

Which of the names that show possession mean but one?

How is each of these made to show possession?

Which of the names that show possession mean more than one?

How is each of these made to show possession?

EXERCISE.

man	woman	child
men	women	children
ox	mouse	goose
oxen	mice	geese

What to See.—Which of these names mean but one?
Which mean more than one?
Do any of these add *s* or *es*?
Notice the words of each pair, and see how they differ.

Copy the following carefully :—

man's home	woman's bonnet
men's homes	women's bonnets
child's toys	ox's horns
children's toys	oxen's horns
mouse's nest	goose's bill
mice's nests	geese's bills

What to See.—Of these helping words showing possession, which mean more than one?

Tell how each of these twelve helping words is made to show possession.

They all show possession in the same way, because no one of them has added *s* or *es* to mean more than one.

When a name has added s *or* es *to denote more than one, the apostrophe alone is joined to show possession.*

To all other names the apostrophe and s *are joined to show possession.*

LESSON LXII.

How to Show Possession — One and More than One.

EXERCISE.

man	child	woman
fox	doll	cricket
girl	boy	pony

What to Do.—Make nine short sentences, using each of the words above to show possession.

Change each of your sentences so as to make this helping name mean more than one, thus—

A child's voice is calling.
Children's voices are calling.

LESSON LXIII.

How to Show Possession — Names, and Words Used for Names.

EXERCISE.

1. A rat washes *its* face.
2. The knife is *his*.
3. The ribbon is *hers*.
4. The rabbits are *ours*.
5. The doves are *yours*.
6. The lambs are *theirs*.

What to See.—What word tells whose face?

What name does *its* take the place of?

Knife is understood after *his*, *ribbon* after *hers*, *rabbits* after *ours*, *doves* after *yours*, and *lambs* after *theirs*.

Notice that, when the words understood are put in, the *s* is dropped from *hers*, *ours*, *yours*, and *theirs*.

Each of these words is a helping word belonging to the word understood and showing possession.

Words that stand for names do not use the apostrophe to show possession.

EXERCISE.

its	his	hers
ours	yours	theirs

What to Do.—Write short sentences, using each of the words above to show possession.

EXERCISE.

oxen	hens	geese
toads	dogs	cows

What to Do.—Write sentences, using the words above to show possession. Then change your sentences so that each of these words shall mean but one.

To the Teacher.—We suggest that the teacher give short sentences orally, pausing for the pupils to put in *his*, *yours*, etc. If quick replies are required, such errors as—

his'n, your'n, etc.,

may be discovered. These will need special attention and drill.

LESSON LXIV.

General Exercises — Quotations.

Copy the following very carefully:—

Grace said, "Yes, sir, I'll try."

Jack said, "No, sir, I can't."

"Yes, ma'am, I'll try," was Julia's prompt answer.

"Yes, sir, if you please," was the boy's reply.

The girl's reply was, "No, sir, I thank you."

What to See.—Explain the contractions *I'll, can't* (not used in formal writing), and *ma'am (madam)*.

Explain all the words that show possession.

Find in each sentence the name of the one addressed, and tell what you have learned about such words.

Notice the word *I* in these sentences.

What have you learned about this word?

QUOTATIONS.

Notice the marks before *yes* and after *try*.

These marks show that the words *yes, sir, I'll try* are not the words of the one who writes the whole sentence, but that they are the exact words of some other person—Grace.

We say that these words are **quoted** from Grace.

In the next sentence what words are quoted from Jack?

These words taken by the writer from some other person we call **Quotations**.

In the third sentence what words are quoted from Julia?

In the fourth what words are quoted from some boy?

In the last what words are quoted from some girl?

Notice that each quotation begins with a capital.

Notice that each quotation is separated from the other words by a comma.

Notice that each quotation has two apostrophes at one end, and two turned-over apostrophes at the other.

These are called **Quotation Marks**.

When a writer uses the exact words of another person, he should inclose them within **Quotation Marks**.

Dictation.

To the Teacher.—Pupils should be able to write these sentences from dictation.

Other similar sentences may be made by the pupils' help, and then dictated.

The time of one or two additional recitations could be very profitably spent here.

LESSON LXV.

General Exercises — Quotations.

Copy the following very carefully:—

Joe's shout, "I'm all right," rang through the forest. The brothers' hunt for "our lost Joe" was over. The boys' sharp call, "Hold on, Ned, we're coming," cheered him. "Now, boys, I've got the rope over him," said Jackson. Ned called up, "O boys! 'tisn't running freely, there's a hitch."

What to See.—Find in the first sentence an apostrophe that helps to show possession, and one that takes the place of *a*.

How are *I am, we are, I have, it is not,* and *there is* contracted?

Tell what the apostrophe stands for in each contraction.

Of the three names showing possession, which mean more than one?

What shows the possession in each?

Notice the word *O* in the last sentence.

What have you learned about writing *O* when it is a word?

What words are here used simply to name the one addressed?

How are these words separated from the others?

What does the mark after *O boys* show?

QUOTATIONS.

Read each quotation.

What do you call the marks before and after each quotation?

Which of these quotations is at the beginning of the sentence?

Which is at the end?

Which are brought in between some of the writer's own words?

If the first quotation is read by itself, will it make sense, like a sentence?

Can you say the same of all the others?

The three words, *our lost Joe,* do not make complete sense, so this quotation does not begin with a capital, and is not separated from the other words by commas.

Does each of the other quotations begin with a capital?

How is each separated from the words it is used with?

Does each quotation in Lesson LXIV. begin with a capital?

Does each make complete sense?

A quotation that makes complete sense begins with a capital, and is generally separated from the other words by a comma or by two commas.

Dictation, etc.

To the Teacher.—The term "quotation" is here used in the sense of "exact quotation." The distinction between direct and indirect quotations should be made farther on.

We suggest that for other lessons the pupils learn to write these sentences correctly from dictation, and that they be able to explain, without the aid of the book, all new points brought out, as well as the points designed for review.

LESSON LXVI.

Putting Sentences Together — Quotations.

THE ANT AND THE GRASSHOPPER—A FABLE.

SEPARATE STATEMENTS.

1. An ant was working.
2. She was making a storehouse.
3. She was filling it.
4. She was tugging a grain of rice.
5. A friend was helping.
6. The grain was bigger than themselves.
7. A grasshopper came up.

STATEMENTS IN PARAGRAPHS.

Copy the following :—

An ant was busy at work one sunny summer day. She was making a storehouse and filling it with food for her family.

Just as she and a friend were tugging along a grain of rice much bigger than themselves, up came a lively grasshopper.

What to See.—Do you think the first sentence above a better beginning for a story than the first of the "separate statements"?

Why?

Tell all you can about the making up of the next sentence.

How many of the "separate statements" are put into the second paragraph above?

Notice that the first words, *just as*, help to hold all the others together, for they keep us anxiously waiting for the words at the end, *Up came a lively grasshopper.*

You may remember being told that, in making a story, it is a good thing to hold the most interesting part for the last, and keep the reader anxious to know how the story is "coming out."

Tell what you can about how the four sentences were put together to make this paragraph.

What to Do.—Now write this story in your own language, and arrange it as you think best.

LESSON LXVII.

Quotations Divided.

Copy the following carefully, noticing the quotation marks very particularly :—

THE ANT AND THE GRASSHOPPER—*Continued.*

" *How do you do, Mother Ant ?* " *said the grasshopper,* " *and why do you work so hard this fine day ?* "

" *O Mr. Grasshopper, I work now so that I may have food when the cold days come.*"

" *Nonsense !* " *replied the grasshopper,* " *you need not be in such a hurry. Summer is not nearly over yet. Come and enjoy yourself as I do.*

" *I do nothing but chirp and dance all day long, while you creep about and think of nothing but work.*"

What to See.—Notice that in this story, or fable, the ant and the grasshopper talk like persons, so you find *Mother Ant* and *Mr. Grasshopper* written as particular names.

Notice that the story is continued from Lesson LXVI.

Notice that the first of these paragraphs is made up of two questions joined by *and*, with *said the grasshopper* thrown in between.

All these words except *said the grasshopper* are one quotation from the grasshopper.

Said the grasshopper divides this quotation, so we mark the part before these words and the part after as if each were a separate quotation.

Tell where you find these quotation marks.

Does this marking leave *said the grasshopper* out of the quotation?

Who is quoted in the next paragraph?

Does the story-writer break into this quotation with any of his own words?

Who is quoted in the next two paragraphs?

What three words of his own does the story-writer throw in here?

How are the marks put so as to leave out these words from the quotation?

The marks before *I* in the last paragraph could be left out, but when the quotation has more than one paragraph, these marks are put before each paragraph to catch the eye and show that the quotation is still going on.

To the Teacher.—Divided quotations and quotations extending through several short paragraphs are very common in books for young children. In order that such stories may be read, copied, and imitated intelligently, it is important that pupils should early be taught all that is brought out above.

Young children can easily be interested in learning about things found in interesting stories.

Let selections containing colloquial quotations be found in Readers or other books and put before the pupils.

After oral exercises have made them familiar with all the points connected with quotations, some of the selections should be dictated for writing, and then compared with the book for correction.

LESSON LXVIII.

Putting Sentences Together — Quotations.

THE ANT AND THE GRASSHOPPER—*Continued.*

SEPARATE STATEMENTS.

1. The summer sun no longer shone.
2. The earth was cold and chill.
3. The grasshopper's wings felt heavy.
4. He did not care to chirp any more.

What to Do.—Dress up these lines as you see fit, and put them into one paragraph.

We do not advise putting them all into one sentence.

Be careful not to make your sentences too long.

Notice how the other part of the story left off. Something about *how long after* might be brought in with the first sentence above.

Copy the following carefully, and notice the quotation marks very particularly :—

Feeling cold and hungry, he said, "I will go and ask Mother Ant to give me something to eat out of that great store of hers."

So he hopped away sadly to the ant's house, and knocked at the door.

" Who is there ?" cried the ant.

" Your friend, the grasshopper."

"*What do you want?*"

"*I have come to beg a little food. I don't know where to get any, and I am very hungry.*"

What to See.—Notice that what you have just copied continues the story from where you left it after joining the sentences at the beginning of this lesson.

Who is quoted in the first paragraph copied?

Where do you find quotation marks?

Are there any quotations in the next paragraph?

Notice that each of the next three lines makes a paragraph.

Notice that the first word of each is set in to the right.

Find each quotation, and tell where the quotation marks are placed.

LESSON LXIX.

Finishing the Fable.

What to Do.—You may finish the story in your own language.

Arrange and connect your sentences as you think best.

HINTS.

What do you think the ant said to the grasshopper?

Do you think she gave him food?

Do you think she said anything about his laughing at her in the summer?

Do you think she mentioned his being lazy, or told him that he might dance all winter?

Do lazy people deserve much help?

What do you think the fable teaches?

LESSON LXX.

Agreement of Chief Parts—General Exercises.

EXERCISE.

1. The rain doesn't stop.
2. The clouds don't move.
3. The weather doesn't please.
4. The flower doesn't open.
5. The grasshopper doesn't chirp.
6. The butterfly doesn't flit.
7. The bee doesn't work.
8. The birds don't sing.
9. The farmer doesn't plough.
10. The children don't shout.
11. The sun doesn't shine.
12. He doesn't care.

What to Do.—Show that *doesn't* and *don't* are correctly written and used in these sentences.

Read the sentences till you can run over them quite rapidly without feeling like putting *don't* or *doesn't* in the wrong place.

EXERCISE.

1. You were beaten.
2. Were you beaten?
3. Weren't you beaten?
4. You were shaken.
5. Weren't you shaken?
6. How you were shaken!
7. We were beaten.
8. Wasn't he beaten?
9. Weren't they beaten?
10. Weren't you chosen?
11. Wasn't he chosen?
12. Weren't we chosen?

What to Do.—Show that each verb above has its right form.

Remember that the verb is always used with you *as if you meant more than one.*

Repeat these sentences quite rapidly till you feel no tendency to use *was* for *were*, or *wasn't* for *weren't*.

LESSON LXXI.

Agreement of Chief Parts—General Exercises.

EXERCISE.

1. There go the rabbits.
2. Here come the dogs.
3. After them goes Joe with his gun.

4. Here come Joe and his dogs on their return.

5. In Joe's bag are a rabbit and a squirrel.

What to See and Do.—We have underlined the subjects in this "exercise."

Find in each sentence the chief word that tells.

Notice that in the third sentence *gun* belongs to a helping phrase, and that in the fourth, *dogs* is one of the chief names.

Show that *go, goes, come,* and *are* are correctly used.

What does *there* do in the first sentence? *Here* in the second? *After them* in the third? *In Joe's bag* in the fifth?

Read these sentences quite rapidly and see whether they sound right.

EXERCISE.

1. The tongs are broken.
2. Aren't the tongs broken?
3. Weren't the tongs broken?
4. Were the scissors stolen?
5. Aren't the shears broken?
6. Have the ashes been shaken?
7. How the ashes do fly!
8. Where were the ashes thrown?
9. Weren't the ashes shaken?
10. Don't the shears cut?

What to Do.—The word *tongs* names one tool; but, as this tool has two parts, the word is written and used as if it meant more than one.

Find other such words.

Show that the proper verb is used in each of these sentences.

Repeat these sentences till you think there is no danger of using the wrong verb.

> **To the Teacher.**—It is hardly probable that your pupils will say *I be, they is*, etc.; but much drill will be required to overcome the use of *don't* for *doesn't*, *was* for *were*—especially with *you*,—and the use of the wrong form of the verb after *there, here*, etc., and with such words as *ashes, tongs*, etc.
>
> It may be necessary to return to these exercises quite frequently. They can be varied in many ways.
>
> Notice that we use the forms *beaten, shaken, chosen, broken, stolen*, etc., for a purpose. It is advisable to bring in such forms incidentally when possible.
>
> Exercises are here suggested on the spelling and use of the homonyms—
>
> > here,   there,
> > hear;   their.

LESSON LXXII.

Agreement of Chief Parts—General Exercises.

To the Teacher.—With the few exceptions noted in the preceding lessons, most failures to make the verb agree with its subject come from not being able to detect these parts immediately and instinctively in whatever part of the sentence they may be found.

The advantage of the earliest possible training in picking out the chief parts, and reading them together in their regular order, is evident.

In constructions like the following, in which the chief parts are transposed, or some word not the subject comes immediately before the verb, the untrained eye and ear are deceived.

In the following "exercise" let the pupils read the chief parts in their natural order, and let the helping words be brought out. It will please the pupils to see why so many persons make mistakes with such sentences.

EXERCISE.

1. On what tree do acorns grow?
2. Here is a pocketful of chestnuts.
3. One of the boys is climbing the tree.
4. In his pocket are a knife and a top.
5. Down come knife, top, and nuts.
6. Every one of the girls has filled her basket.
7. Neither of the bags has been filled.
8. Halloo! doesn't that squirrel know how to crack nuts!
9. Weren't you and Billy up the tree?
10. A whole barrelful of nuts was taken from here yesterday.

What to See and Do.—We have marked the chief parts of each sentence. You may read them together, putting the subject before its verb.

In the third sentence *one* means *one boy,* and *of the boys* is only a helping phrase.

In the sixth, *one* means *one girl.*

In the seventh, *neither* means *neither bag.*

Read each sentence till you think there is no danger of using the wrong verb.

Dictation.

To the Teacher.—For another lesson, these sentences may be varied, and dictated with the test word omitted, to be filled in by the pupils afterward.

LESSON LXXIII.

Addresses — Dates — Names — Titles.

Copy the following and notice everything :—

Noah D. Choate, Esq.,
Milford,
New Haven Co.,
Conn.

Rev. Jonathan Wesley, D.D.,
Hot Springs,
Garland Co.,
Ark.

Edwin F. Holmes, M. D.,
550 Chestnut St.,
Philadelphia,
Pa.

What to See.—In these addresses are found the abbreviations of *Connecticut, Arkansas, Pennsylvania,* and *Esquire.*

Tell how each is made.

What do you mean by a person's address? (See Lesson XXXIV.)

Notice in the first address that the title is put after the name.

This title is given to lawyers, and to other prominent persons.

How is this abbreviation separated from the name?

What do you find after each line of this address?

What two reasons can you give for the period after *Conn.?*

The name in the second address has one title before and another after it.

You learned about *Rev.* in Lesson XXXIII.

Colleges sometimes give clergymen the title of **Doctor of Divinity.**

The abbreviation for this title is **D.D.**

In speaking to this clergyman, or of him, you would say *Doctor Wesley*.

His name may also be written—

Rev. Dr. Jonathan Wesley.

Doctor of Medicine is abbreviated **M.D.**
This is the title of one that practices medicine and heals diseases.

The third name may also be written—

Dr. Edwin F. Holmes.

Be careful not to use both **Mr.** *and* **Esq.** *with the same name;* as—

Mr. John Smith, Esq.   (Very bad.)

Do not use either **Mr.** *or* **Esq.** *with* **Dr., M.D.,** *or* **D.D.**

Notice that the first address gives the name and title, the post-office, the county, and the state.

The third address gives the name and title, the number of the house, the street, the city, and the state.

What two things just named are put together without a comma?

Tell what is given in each script line of these addresses.

Tell what each comma separates.

It may be well for you to see whether you remember what was learned in Lessons XXXIV. and XXXV.

Dictation.

To the Teacher.—Let the pupils write the addresses from dictation. Question them closely on every part.

LESSON LXXIV.

Addresses, Dates, Etc.

EXERCISES—ADDRESSES.

Master Ralph S. Lee lives in the city of San Francisco, which is in California. The number of his house is 777. It is in Van Ness Avenue.

Miss Agnes Harrison is staying at the Southern Hotel, in the city of St. Louis. This city is in Missouri.

Philip C. Hayne, a lawyer, lives in the city of Charleston, in the state of South Carolina. His house is numbered 75. It is in Meeting Street.

Robert O. Bryant is a Doctor of Medicine. He lives at Harper's Ferry, in Jefferson County. This county is in West Virginia.

Paul J. Calvin is a Doctor of Divinity, living at Genoa, in Nebraska. Genoa is in Nance County.

What to Do.—From the five groups of statements above write out five addresses in the proper form.

You may write the last two titles in two ways.

In the second address the name of the hotel takes the place of the house number and the street.

We here give you the abbreviations for the states mentioned in these addresses:—

Cal., Mo., S. C., W. Va., Nebr.

To the Teacher.—Attention may be called to the use of *at* and *in*, and the expression *staying at the Southern Hotel* may be noted as preferred to *stopping*, etc.

Dictation.

The pupils should be able to write these addresses from dictation till they are correct in every particular.

This dictation, with the exercises on dates, may require a separate lesson.

EXERCISES—DATES.

The telegraph came into use in the United States on the twenty-seventh day of May, in the year eighteen hundred and forty-four.

The Pilgrims landed on the twenty-first day of December, in the year sixteen hundred and twenty.

Washington became our first president on the thirtieth day of April, in the year seventeen hundred and eighty-nine.

What to Do.—Write out the dates mentioned above in the short form given in Lesson XXXVIII.

After writing these dates, read them as directed in Lesson XXXVIII.

LESSON LXXV.

A Letter.

Copy the following letter very carefully, and notice everything :—

1001 Canal St.,
New Orleans, La.,
Feb. 21, 1892.

My dear Edith,

Last Wednesday was my ninth birthday. Fanny Calhoun, Laura Davis, and Marian Macaulay spent the afternoon with me, and I think no four girls ever had a happier time.

My friends were very kind to me. Among my presents are three books with which I am delighted. They are Mrs. Burnett's "Little Lord Fauntleroy," Dickens's "A Child's History of England," and Miss Alcott's "Little Women".

Always your friend,
Cora Carlyle.

Miss Edith Lincoln,
Albion,
Dane Co.,
Wis.

STAMP

What to See and Do.—The comma between *me* and *and*, in the second paragraph of the letter, separates two sentences that have been joined by *and*.

The comma between *books* and *with*, in the third paragraph, separates two sentences that have been joined by *which*.

For a review you may tell what all the other commas do.

Tell about the abbreviations and the periods.

La. stands for *Louisiana*, and **Wis.** for *Wisconsin*.

Find three particular names inclosed by quotation marks. These are names, or titles, of books.

Without these marks you might take *Little Lord Fauntleroy* as the name of a real person, instead of a title quoted from Mrs. Burnett's book.

Pick out all the particular names.

Draw the outline of an envelope and write the address in proper form.

LESSON LXXVI.

An Original Letter.

What to Do.—Write to some friend and tell about your last birthday.

If you can remember nothing of importance that happened, tell what you expect to do, or would like to do, on your next birthday.

Put all parts of your letter in the proper form.

Group your sentences into paragraphs.

LESSON LXXVII.

Copy the following very carefully:—

> Brandon, Rutland Co., Vt.,
> May 10, 1891.
>
> My dear Mamma;
>   I am so glad that our visit to Uncle Abram's farm was changed from summer to spring. Yesterday Aunt Mary took Alice and me into the woods for a walk. We were soon under the grand old trees, and, O mamma! what a sweet, woodsy fragrance

filled the air! It was so unlike the air of New York!

All at once the quiet of the woods was broken by a sharp rap! rap! rap!

"Who is that rapping?" whispered Alice.

"That," said Aunt Mary, "is a woodpecker tapping the old beech tree yonder. He is getting out a fat grub for his breakfast."

After listening to the birds' clear, sweet voices a while, we went on into the woods. But, dear mamma, I must stop here, although I have just begun my story.

    Your loving daughter,
      Bessie.

    Mrs. Walter R. Webb,
     49 West 25th St.,
      New York City.

To the Teacher.—Pupils should be able to write this letter from dictation. They may correct their own or each other's work by comparison with the book.

LESSON LXXVIII.

General Exercises.

What to See.—What are separated by the commas found in the lines before and after the body of the letter in Lesson LXXVII.?

Explain the use of the capitals and the periods in this letter.

The first *I* is a capital for what two reasons? (See Lesson XXXIX.)

Find the names of two seasons.

Do they begin with capitals?

Explain the exclamation marks.

Where are commas used with the name of the one addressed?

What quotations do you find in this letter?

Is either of these divided into parts by some of the writer's own words?

Tell how these quotations are marked.

What words in this letter show possession?

Explain their forms.

How many paragraphs in the body of this letter?

How are paragraphs made?

To the Teacher.—Call attention to the order of the words *Alice* and *me*, and to the form of *me*. Exercises are here suggested showing that such terms as "*Alice* and *I*" are used as subjects, and that such as "*Alice* and *me*" are used after the verb to tell whom.

LESSON LXXIX.

An Original Letter.

What to Do. —You may write another letter for Bessie, and tell the rest of her story. (See Lesson LXXVII.)

Perhaps you prefer to tell about another walk this little party took along a pleasant stream. If you wish, you may use these—

HINTS.

Ripple over pebbles — leap over rocks—a sound like laughter—dance and whirl on—deep clear pool—alders and willow bend over—catkins, pussy willows — trout leap — green sloping banks—white and blue violets—What other wild flowers? — Took home what?

LESSON LXXX.

An Original Letter.

HINTS.

Frank Harper visits his grandfather at Hanover, Grafton Co., N. H. (New Hampshire).

He is interested in the pigs, the calves, the cows, and the pony. He watches the man plowing, and notices the birds following the plow to pick up insects. He finds a bird's nest.

Frank writes to his brother Albert, who is staying at the Palmer House, Chicago, and tells him what he has seen and done.

What to Do.—You may write Frank's letter.

A GATHERING UP.

To the Teacher.—See "To the Teacher," p. 36.

Names are made to mean more than one by adding s or es.

Some names ending with y change the y to ie when s is added.

If a, e, or o is before the y, s is added without changing the y.

When a name has added s or es to denote more than one, the apostrophe alone is joined to show possession.

To all other names the apostrophe and s are joined to show possession.

Words that stand for names do not use the apostrophe to show possession; as, **his, hers, its, ours, yours, theirs.**

Contractions.

I'll, can't, ma'am, I'm,
we're, I've, 'tisn't, there's.

His'n, your'n, their'n, etc., are incorrect.

When a writer uses the exact words of another person, he should inclose them within Quotation Marks.

When a writer divides a quotation by putting in words of his own, each part of the quotation should be inclosed.

When a quotation makes complete sense, it begins with a Capital, *and is generally separated from the other words by a* Comma *or by two commas.*

To the Teacher.—See " To the Teacher," p. 127.

Abbreviations.

Esq., Esquire.
D.D., Doctor of Divinity.
M.D., Doctor of Medicine.
Ark., Arkansas.
Cal., California.
S. C., South Carolina.
Nebr., Nebraska.
Wis., Wisconsin.

N. H., New Hampshire.
Conn., Connecticut.
Pa., Pennsylvania.
Mo., Missouri.
W. Va., West Virginia.
La., Louisiana.
Vt., Vermont.

Be careful not to use both Mr. *and* Esq. *with the same name.*

Do not use either Mr. *or* Esq. *with* Dr., M.D., *or* D.D.

PART SECOND.

To the Teacher.—Between the lessons on the verb the teacher may, if variety is needed, introduce lessons in composition and letter-writing selected from the pages farther on.

Lessons in letter-writing should be given at frequent intervals.

The teacher will find opportunity for continuing the incidental exercises on homonyms. For example—page 154, *see* and *sea;* page 160, *blew* and *blue, know* and *no, knew* and *new;* page 161, *beat* and *beet, break* and *brake, write* and *right, wrote* and *rote;* page 164, *rode* and *rowed;* page 165, *steal* and *steel,* etc.

LESSON LXXXI.

Using the Verb Right.

Do, did, done.

EXERCISE.

1. We *do* the work to-day.
2. We *did* the work yesterday.
3. We *have done* the work to-day.

To use *done* for *did* in the second sentence above would be very bad.

Done *must never be used by itself as the chief part that tells.*

EXERCISE.

1. Who *did* the mischief?
2. The wind *did* it.
3. The frost *did* it.
4. The cat *did* it.
5. Who *did* wrong?
6. I *did* wrong.
7. Tom *did* right.
8. I *did* it carelessly.
9. Tom *did* his best.
10. Who *did* up the package?
11. John *did* up the package.
12. Mary *did* her work very neatly.

What to Do.—Read these sentences till you think that there is no danger of your using *done* for *did*.

Make five sentences, using *did* as a complete verb.

See, saw, seen.

EXERCISE.

1. We *see* it now.
2. We *saw* it yesterday.
3. We *have seen* it.

To use *seen* for *saw* in the second sentence would be very bad.

Seen *must never be used by itself as the chief part that tells.*

EXERCISE.

1. I *saw* him this morning.
2. I *saw* him when he *did* it.
3. Jack *saw* him, and *did* his best to catch him.
4. The boys *saw* the storm coming.
5. The crow *saw* me before I *saw* him.

What to Do.—Read these sentences till the verbs sound natural, and there is no danger of using *seen* for *saw*.

Make five sentences using *saw* correctly.

To the Teacher.—That the pupil's eye, ear, and tongue may be trained together, it is better, in all these sentences for repetition, to have the full form in the text-book. For further drill the teacher may put these or similar sentences on the board, leaving blanks to be filled.

LESSON LXXXII.

Using the Right Verb — *Lie* and *Lay*.

EXERCISE.

1. The dolls *lie* on the floor.
2. They *lay* there yesterday.
3. They have *lain* there all day.

What to See.—In the first sentence *lie* tells what the dolls do now, or at the *present*.

In the second, *lay* tells what the dolls did in the *past*—yesterday.

In the third, notice that *lain* follows *have*. It can not be used alone as a chief part.

Lie, *lay*, and *lain* are three forms of the same verb.

We may call *lie* the *present* form, *lay* the *past* form, and *lain* the form used with *have*, *had*, etc.

EXERCISE.

1. We *lay* our books on the table now.
2. We *laid* them on the shelf yesterday.
3. We have *laid* them away carefully.

What to See.—In the first sentence *lay* tells what we do now, or at the *present*.

In the second, *laid* tells what we did in the past—yesterday.

In the third, *laid* is used with *have*.

Lay and *laid* are forms of the same verb.

Lay is the *present*, and *laid* is the *past*. *Laid* is also used after *have*, *had*, etc.

HOW *Lie* AND *Lay* DIFFER IN MEANING.

Present.	Past.	Used with *have*, etc.
Lie,	lay,	lain.
Lay,	laid,	laid.

Lie means *to rest* or *recline*.

Lay means *to put* or *place*.

Do not use lay *for* lie, nor laid *for* lay *and* lain.

What to Do.—Put *rest* or *rested* in place of *lie, lay,* and *lain* in the sentences of the first "exercise."

Use *recline* or *reclined* in the same sentences.

Use *put* in place of *lay* and *laid* in the sentences of the second "exercise."

Now use *place* or *placed* in the same sentences.

Write the first sentence of each "exercise" and use for the subject a *name* that means but one.

Read the sentences of both "exercises" till the verbs sound familiar.

Make sentences using *lie*, *lay*, and *lain*.

Make sentences using *lay* (to place) and *laid*.

LESSON LXXXIII.

Using the Right Verb — *Sit* and *Set*.

EXERCISE.

1. The dolls *sit* in their chairs.
2. They *sat* there yesterday.
3. They have *sat* there all day.

What to See.—In the first sentence *sit* tells what the dolls do now, or at the *present*.

In the second, *sat* tells what the dolls did in the *past*—yesterday.

In the third, *sat* is used with *have*.

Sit and *sat* are forms of the same verb.

Sit is the *present*, and *sat* is the *past*. *Sat* is also used after *have*, etc.

EXERCISE.

1. We now *set* the dolls' chairs by the table.
2. We *set* them there last week.
3. We had *set* them there before.

What to See.—In the first sentence *set* tells what we do now, or at the *present*.

In the second, *set* tells what we did in the *past*—last week.

In the third, *set* is used after *had*.

The same word *set* is used for the *present*, the *past*, and with *have*, *had*, etc.

HOW *Sit* AND *Set* DIFFER IN MEANING.

Present.	Past.	Used with *have*, etc.
Sit,	sat,	sat.
Set,	set,	set.

Sit means *to rest*.
Set means *to put* or *place*.
Do not use set *for* sit *and* sat.

What to Do.—Put *rest* or *rested* in place of *sit* and *sat* in the sentences of the first "exercise."

Use *put* in place of *set* in the sentences of the second "exercise."

Use *place* or *placed* in the same sentences.

Write the first sentence of each "exercise" and use for the subject a *name* that means but one.

LESSON LXXXIV.

General Exercises—*Lie* and *Lay*, *Sit* and *Set*.

EXERCISE.

1. *Lie* down, Carlo.
2. You have *lain* long enough.
3. How quietly you have *lain!*

4. Now *sit* up.
5. *Lay* your right paw in my hand.
6. You have *laid* down the left.
7. Now *lie* down where you *lay* before.
8. Are you tired of *lying* there ?
9. Now *sit* for your picture.
10. You have *sat* long enough.
11. How patiently you have *sat!*
12. Bring that stick and *lay* it down here.
13. Let it *lie*.
14. Now *lay* it where it *lay* before.
15. Take this basket and *set* it on the stool.
16. Let it *sit* there.
17. Now *set* it where it *sat* before.
18. You may *lie* on the rug.
19. Have you *lain* long enough ?
20. Carlo *lies* down or *sits* up, as I tell him.
21. I told Rover to *lie* down, and he *sat* up.
22. I told him to *sit* up, and he *lay* down.

What to Do.—Repeat these sentences till there is no danger of using the wrong verb.

To the Teacher.—No instruction in technical grammar is needed here.

The pupils may be allowed to test the italicized words above by putting in their stead *rest* or *rested*, *place* or *placed*.

It may help in these tests to explain that when one is standing, we say, *Sit down* = *Rest with the body partly down;* and when one is lying, we say, *Sit up* = *Rest with the body partly up.* *Lie down* = *Rest with the body down.*

Dictation.

These sentences may be dictated with the test words omitted.

Sentences written by the pupils should be mainly those using *lie, lay,* and *lain.*

Several recitations can profitably be spent here.

LESSON LXXXV.

Using the Verb Right.

Present.	Past.	Used with *have*, etc.
Blow,	blew,	blown.
Draw,	drew,	drawn.
Grow,	grew,	grown.
Know,	knew,	known.
Throw,	threw,	thrown.

Remember that blew, blown; drew, drawn; grew, grown; knew, known; threw, thrown, *are correct forms, and that blowed, drawed, growed, knowed, throwed are incorrect forms.*

EXERCISE.

1. The wind *blew* hard in the night.
2. Large oaks *were blown* down.
3. The snail *drew* back his feelers.
4. He *has drawn* his slimy body across the walk.
5. This flower *grew* by the roadside.
6. The vine *has grown* over the trellis.

7. He *knew* every wild flower by name.
8. I *have known* him for years.
9. Tall trees *threw* their shadows across the field.
10. The ant-hill *was* suddenly *thrown* into confusion.

What to Do.—Read the verb in each sentence, and tell which form is used.

Read the sentences till the verbs sound familiar.

Write ten sentences, using the words in the second and third columns.

ORAL EXERCISE.

Has blown, have been blown, was blown, have blown, were blown.

What to Do.—Read these verbs, and put a proper subject before each.

Repeat this exercise, using *drawn, grown, known, thrown* in place of *blown.*

Put three subjects before each verb in the second column at the beginning of the lesson.

LESSON LXXXVI.
Using the Verb Right.

Present.	Past.	Used with *have*, etc.
Beat,	beat,	beaten.
Break,	broke,	broken.
Fall,	fell,	fallen.
Freeze,	froze,	frozen.
Write,	wrote,	written.

Do not use **beat** *for* **beaten, broke** *for* **broken, fell** *for* **fallen, froze** *for* **frozen, wrote** *for* **written.**

EXERCISE.

1. You *have beaten* me fairly.
2. This writing *can* not easily *be beaten.*
3. The wind *has broken* the branches.
4. Many of the willows *were broken.*
5. The balloon *has fallen* into the lake.
6. All the tender buds *have been frozen.*
7. He *has* always *written* promptly.
8. No letter *could be* more carefully *written.*

What to Do.—Read the verb in each sentence and tell which form is used.

Tell what the helping words that come between the parts of the verb do.

Read the sentences till the verbs sound natural.

Write ten sentences, using each of the words in the second and third columns.

ORAL EXERCISE.

Has beaten, had beaten, have beaten, is beaten, are beaten, was beaten, were beaten, will be beaten, may be beaten, might be beaten, cannot be beaten, could be beaten.

What to Do.—Read these verbs with a proper subject before each.

Repeat these exercises, using instead of *beaten* the words *broken, fallen, frozen,* and *written.*

LESSON LXXXVII.

Using the Verb Right.

Present.	Past.	Used with *have*, etc.
Choose,	chose,	chosen.
Drive,	drove,	driven.
Fly,	flew,	flown.
Give,	gave,	given.
Go,	went,	gone.

Do not use chose *for* chosen, drove *for* driven, flew *for* flown, gave *for* given, went *for* gone.

What to Do.—Make five oral sentences, using each of the words in the second column to tell what is past.

Write ten sentences, using one of the following verbs in each: *has chosen, was chosen, have driven, were driven, have flown, had flown, has given, was given, have gone, had gone.*

Make oral sentences, using *is, are, has been, have been, will be, may be,* and *should be,* before *chosen, driven,* and *given.*

Make oral sentences, using *has, may have, must have, might have,* and *could have,* before *flown* and *gone.*

Use some form of *lie* or *lay* in place of each of the following words in italics: "The snow *remains* on the mountain." "It *remained* there all summer." "The wings *rest* over the back." "The wings are *put* over the back."

LESSON LXXXVIII.

Using the Verb Right.

PRESENT.	PAST.	USED WITH *have*, ETC.
Ride,	rode,	ridden.
Shake,	shook,	shaken.
Speak,	spoke,	spoken.
Forsake,	forsook,	forsaken.
Rise,	rose,	risen.

Do not use rode *for* ridden, shook *for* shaken, spoke *for* spoken, forsook *for* forsaken, rose *for* risen.

What to Do.—Make five oral sentences, using each of the words in the second column to tell what is past.

Write ten sentences, using one of the following verbs in each : *have ridden, could be ridden, were shaken, should be shaken, has spoken, had spoken, was forsaken, have forsaken, has risen, had risen.*

Make oral sentences, using *has been, have been, must be, may have been,* before *ridden, shaken, spoken,* and *forsaken.*

Make oral sentences, using *have, must have,* and *should have,* before *risen.*

Raise or *raised* is sometimes used by mistake for the forms of *rise* or *arise.*

Do not say, "He *raised* up;" but say, "He *arose*," or "He *raised* himself up."

Do not say, "The fog *raised;*" but, "The fog *rose.*"

LESSON LXXXIX.

Using the Verb Right.

Present.	Past.	Used with *have*, etc.
Steal,	stole,	stolen.
Take,	took,	taken.
Tear,	tore,	torn.
Wear,	wore,	worn.

Do not use stole *for* stolen, took *for* taken, tore *for* torn, wore *for* worn.

What to Do.—Write ten sentences, using the words in the second and third columns correctly.

Make ten oral sentences, using the words in the third column correctly.

Present.	Past.	Used with *have*, etc.
Come,	came,	come.
Drown,	drowned,	drowned.
Attack,	attacked,	attacked.

What to Do.—Make oral sentences, using *come* and *came.* Be sure to use *came*, not *come*, to tell what is past.

Make oral sentences, using *drowned* and *attacked.*

Be sure to pronounce *drowned* in one syllable, and *attacked* in two syllables, not three. Pronounce *ed* in *attacked* like *t.*

LESSON XC.

Helping Words Joined to Names.

Hints for Word Pictures.

Copy the following sentences :—

1. Large, feathery snowflakes are floating through the air.
2. Bright, cheerful fires are crackling on the hearth.
3. Five lively little chickadees have come for their supper.
4. A beautiful white blanket is spread over the field.
5. The bare, brown branches of the trees are ridged with pearl.
6. Each tall, tapering pine is wrapped in a pure, white cloak.
7. The world is changed into a new, strange, white world.

What to See.—In each of the sentences above the verb is made up of two words. Find each verb.

Put *what* before each verb and find the chief name.

The name *snowflakes* brings up a picture in your mind, but notice how much clearer this picture is made by the helping words *large* and *feathery*.

What helping words are joined to *fires?*

Do they make the picture more distinct?

What helping words are joined to *chickadees?*

Tell what helping words are joined to the chief name in each of the other sentences.

A, in the fourth sentence, means about the same as *one*.

The, in the fifth, points out, somewhat as you would point out the branches with your finger if they were really before you.

Other names besides the chief names have helping words.

In the last sentence, find a name in the helping phrase joined to *is changed*.

What four helping words are joined to this name?

Notice that some of the helping words in these sentences are separated by the comma, and some are not.

Notice that when the comma is used, a short pause is naturally made, and that when no comma is used, the helping words read together closely.

See whether the comma takes the place of *and*.

LESSON XCI.

Helping Words Joined to Names.

Hints for Word Pictures.

EXERCISE.

1. A bright, sunny landscape.
2. Gay, sparkling frostwork.
3. Queer little tracks in the snow.
4. The merry tinkling sleigh bells.
5. Laughing, shouting voices.
6. Delightful long winter evenings.

7. Poor little boys and girls.
8. No thick, warm clothes.
9. No happy, cheerful home.

What to See.—Are these word pictures sentences? Why?

Which is the name, and which are the helping words in each?

Show by your reading of each where the comma should be used.

Between which helping words could *and* be put?

Which helping words are put together without a comma?

What do you here learn about the comma?

A Winter Day.

What to Do.—Make a connected story of two or more paragraphs, telling about some winter day. Use as many words or sentences from the two preceding "exercises" as you wish.

Be sure that every "helping" word does really help.

LESSON XCII.

Helping Words Joined to Names—Composition.

The Old Log Water-trough.

Pleasant road through *an old* forest. Sit under *swaying* boughs. Listen to *a scolding* squirrel among *the sunny* leaves. Music of *a tiny crystal* stream. Shoots along *a mossy* grove. Drops with *a rippling, laughing* sound into *the old log* water-trough. *Velvet* clumps of *deep-green* moss. *Trailing* vines and *delicate* sprays. *Flickering* shadows of *the overhanging* beech. *Weary, dusty* traveler. *Hot, dry* lips. *Cool, delicious* draught.

What to Do.—Tell what each of these italicized words helps to picture.

Imagine yourself sitting by this old forest road, with the water-trough before you, and then tell what you see and hear. You need not confine yourself to these hints. Make such changes and additions as you choose.

Put your thoughts into a smooth, connected story.

Do not use any word that does not really help.

LESSON XCIII.

Helping Words Joined to Names.

EXERCISE.

An aged man; *an* east wind; *an* idle boy; *an* old forest; *an* unkind remark; *an* apple; *an* egg; *an* insect; *an* orange; *an* uncle; *an* hour; *an* honest man; *a* unit; *a* useful tool.

What to See and Do.—*An* and *aged* are both joined to *man*; but if we take away *aged*, *an* drops its *n*, for *an man* would not sound right.

Read each of the first five groups of words, and tell what sound comes immediately after *an*.

Read each of these groups, and omit the second helping word.

Read each of the other groups, and tell what sound comes immediately after *an* or *a*.

Notice that *h* in *hour* and *honest* is not sounded, and that *unit* and *useful* begin with the sound of *y*.

An is used before the sounds of *a, e, i, o, u;* and *a,* before other sounds.

EXERCISE.

That sort of people ; *this sort* of people ; *that kind* of books ; *this kind* of books.

Those ashes ; these ashes ; those scissors ; these scissors ; those tongs ; these tongs.

We walked *four miles* an hour. The wall was *two feet* thick. The farmer sold *two bushels* of apples, *three barrels* of potatoes, and *five pounds* of maple sugar.

What to See and Do.—Notice the helping words and the names in italics.

Which helping words belong to names that mean one?

Which belong to names that mean more than one?

Read these expressions till all the helping words sound familiar.

Explain the use of the commas in the last sentence of the " exercise."

This *and* **that** *are used with names that denote one; and* **these, those, two, three,** *etc., with names that denote more than one.*

EXERCISE.

Those crows are pulling up the corn. *Those* grapes are sour. Please pass *those* oranges. Set *those* idle fellows at work.

What to See and Do.—With what kind of names is *those* used?

Would *them* sound right in place of *those?*

Read these sentences and see whether they sound right.

Do not use them *for* those.

To the Teacher.—Confine the drill to those forms that are liable to misuse.

Time is often wasted in exercises on forms that pupils never use incorrectly.

If a thorough test shows that no pupils are in the habit of saying *a apple, a orange,* etc., the first "exercise" should be briefly treated. Certainly there is no danger of using *an man, an boy,* etc.

The misuse of *these* and *those* is confined chiefly to the nouns *sort* and *kind.* Pupils will not say *these boy, these man;* nor *this sorts, that kinds.*

Where the pupils are found deficient, the exercises should be dictated with blanks, then extended, and frequently reviewed.

LESSON XCIV.

Helping Words Joined to Verbs.

Hints for Word Pictures.

EXERCISE.

1. The snow is *now* falling *fast.*
2. The wind drives it *here.*

3. The wind drives it *there*.
4. The wind drives it *up*.
5. The wind drives it *down*.
6. The wind drives it *round*.
7. The snow and wind frolic *merrily*.

What to See.—We have italicized the words that help by telling *how*, *when*, and *where*.

What word helps *is falling* by telling *when*?
What word helps *is falling* by telling *how*?
Find five words, each of which helps its verb by telling *where*.
What does *merrily* tell?

JOINING SENTENCES.

Copy the following:—

Now the snow is falling *fast;* and, as it falls, the wind drives it *here* and *there, up* and *down, round* and *round,* in wild dances. The snow and wind frolic *together merrily.*

What to See.—Notice that from the third, fourth, fifth, and sixth sentences we have taken only the words *there, up, down,* and *round.*

Why can the other words be omitted without losing the meaning?

What other changes do you find?

Notice that some of the helping words are here put in pairs.

How are the pairs separated?

EXERCISE.

1. *Here* comes a party of boys and girls.
2. The wind blows *fiercely*.
3. They are *snugly* tucked under warm robes.
4. The bells jingle *merrily*.
5. The horses toss their heads *impatiently*.
6. *Away* they dash.
7. *Soon* they plunge into a snowbank.
8. *Over* goes the sleigh.

What to See.—We have italicized the words that help by telling *how*, *when*, and *where*.

Find four words that tell *how* the action was done.

Find one word that helps by telling *when*.

Find three italicized words that help by telling *where*.

Which of these helping words are placed at the beginning of the sentence?

Can you find other places for these words?

Which arrangement do you prefer?

To the Teacher.—Let the pupils see that in Lessons XC. and XCI. a quiet fall of snow and a quiet winter scene are pictured, and that in this lesson a scene is presented in which there is much action.

As a preparation for the next lesson, the pupils may vary and combine orally the sentences of the "exercise" above, and then continue the story.

Encourage each pupil to suggest some incident. In discussing the different expressions let the pupils help to decide which sound best. The arrangement should also be discussed.

LESSON XCV.

Helping Words Joined to Verbs — Composition.

ONE STORMY WINTER DAY.

What to Do.—Write a short story of two or more paragraphs, telling what happened on a stormy winter day.

Take what you choose from the two "exercises" in the preceding lesson.

Underline the words that tell *how, when,* or *where.*

To the Teacher.—The pupils should not be held closely to pointing out all adverbs.

LESSON XCVI.

Phrases Joined to the Chief Parts.

Hints for Word Pictures.

A SQUIRREL'S MORNING RUN.

1. A barking, scolding sound is heard *from the tree.*
2. Two black eyes appear *at a knot-hole.*
3. An empty nut rattles *to the ground.*
4. A red squirrel scurries down *through the branches.*
5. He leaps *upon the fence.*
6. Away he goes *with flying colors.*
7. Suddenly he halts and springs *into an apple tree.*
8. A tumult is heard *among the bees.*
9. Down comes a mimic snow-fall *of blossoms.*

***What to See.*—**Notice that the phrases are in italics.

In each of the sentences except the last read the verb and its helping phrase together.

Which of these phrases help by telling *where?*

Find the subject in the ninth sentence.

What does the phrase *of blossoms* do?

In the first sentence, see whether *from* or *the* or *tree*, taken alone, would help *is heard.*

You see that the words of a phrase, all taken together, are like a single helping word.

Find the chief parts in each sentence.

Find all the helping words, and tell what they do.

LESSON XCVII.

Phrases Joined to the Chief Parts.

Hints for Word Pictures.

A Squirrel's Morning Run—*Continued.*

1. Again he is dashing *down the fence.*
2. He clears a certain rail *with one long jump.*
3. *Under this rail* hangs a hornet's nest.
4. He finds a woodpecker's den *in a dead tree.*
5. Madam is *at home.*
6. She delivers a pickax blow *between his eyes.*
7. Away he speeds *with whisking tail.*
8. He looks wistfully *at a robin's nest.*
9. His appetite *for birds' eggs* has been spoiled.

What to See.—Notice that the phrases are in italics.

In each of the sentences except the last, read the verb and its helping phrase together.

What does the phrase *for birds' eggs* do?

Notice that the last word in each phrase is a name, and that helping words are sometimes joined to it.

Find all such helping words, and tell what they do.

The first word in each phrase is the connecting word.

Explain the possessive names found in these sentences.

To the Teacher.—Oral work may be needed in preparation for the following lesson.

LESSON XCVIII.

Phrases — Composition.

A Squirrel's Morning Run.

What to Do.—Make a connected story of the sentences given in the two preceding lessons.

You may make any changes and additions that will help your story.

Underline some of your phrases, and tell what they do.

LESSON XCIX.

Using Helping Words Right.

Be careful not to put together helping words or phrases that have the same meaning; as, "a short little word."

EXERCISE.

Small, tiny ; verdant, green ; great, large, big; promptly, without hesitation ; in perfect silence, without the slightest noise.

What to Do.—Tell which of these helping words or phrases should not be used together. Why ?

Use each with a name or a verb.

Be careful to get the right helping word.

EXERCISE.

Elegant manners, furniture, dress, house.
Splendid sunset, palace, jewels, victory.
Awful storm, roar, crash.
Lovely woman, face, child.
Horrible story, crime, pit.
Excellent, delicious, pretty, neat, ugly, homely.

What to See and Do.—Repeat each of the first five helping words with each name that follows it.

These helping words are much misused.

It is not right to say, "perfectly *elegant, splendid,* or *lovely* pie, cake, or butter."

What two words in the last line of the "exercise" may describe "pie, cake, butter," etc.?

It is wrong to talk about a "perfectly *awful* or *horrible* bonnet or shoe."

What words in the last line of the "exercise" may describe a bonnet or a shoe ?

Find other names to which each of the italicized words of the " exercise " may be joined.

Do not use most *for* almost *or* nearly, real *for* really *or* very, bad *for* badly, good *for* well.

EXERCISE.
1. *Almost* every boy was shouting.
2. I have *almost* finished.
3. *Really* honest men can be found.
4. Did you sleep *well?*
5. I slept *badly.*

What to See and Do.—Some words may be joined to either a verb or another helping word. *Almost* in the first sentence is joined to *every ;* in the second, to *have finished.*

Real, bad, and *good* are joined to names.

Read the sentences of this "exercise" till they sound familiar.

Such expressions as "*real* smart man," "*most* all of it," "act *bad*," "writes *good*," are incorrect.

Write correct sentences showing what is meant by these expressions.

To the Teacher.—The sentences given here and those made by the pupils may be dictated with the test words omitted.

LESSON C.
Using Helping Words Right.

Put helping words where they will give the right meaning and sound best.

EXERCISE.

1. *Here* we were told our friends had waited an hour.
2. We talked about sailing around the world *in the evening*.
3. A boy is wanted on a farm *of steady habits*.
4. He took a severe cold during the journey *on his lungs*.
5. Peter Grant died while eating breakfast *seventy-five years old*.

What to See and Do.—From the position of *here*, the first sentence may have either of two meanings. Bring out each of these meanings clearly.

Make the other sentences clear by putting the italicized words and phrases in the best place.

Do not use two denying words where the meaning needs but one.

EXERCISE.

1. I have none.
2. I haven't any.
3. He is doing nothing.
4. He isn't doing anything.
5. There are no ghosts.
6. There aren't any ghosts.
7. It can be found nowhere.
8. It can't be found anywhere.
9. I have seen nothing.
10. I haven't seen anything.

What to See and Do.—If you mean, "I have *none*," you certainly would not say, "I *haven't none*," for this would be a very awkward way of saying, "I have some."

Find the denying word in each sentence of the "exercise."

Tell which sentences have the same meaning.

What mistakes have you heard in such sentences?

Read the sentences of the "exercise," and notice whether they sound natural.

To the Teacher.—By questions and various devices, get the pupils to use sentences containing negatives. Let them see the absurdity of making one negative contradict another unless they wish to affirm. Let them see that two negatives are sometimes intentionally used to affirm; as, "*No* man can do *nothing*."

LESSON CI.

A Study of Sentences.

To the Teacher.—Let special attention be given to arrangement and to points brought out in the preceding lessons. Let some of the work be written.

THE GAY BUTTERFLY.

1. For a few weeks or months the butterfly flits in the sunshine among the flowers.
2. The butterfly's happy life in the sunshine among the flowers lasts only for a few weeks or months.
3. Have not the earth, the sky, and the sea given all their gayest tints to the butterfly?

4. How beautifully the colors are put together in spots, streaks, and rich borders!

5. On the butterfly's gorgeous wings look for all the colors of the rainbow.

6. He goes through the air with a zig-zag motion.

7. This gay creature of the sunshine is seldom seen on the wing before nine in the morning.

8. Long before sunset he steals away under the leaves.

What to See and Do.—Find the two chief words in the first sentence.

Find a phrase that helps *flits* by telling how long.

Find two phrases that help by telling where.

Arrange these phrases in several ways, and tell which way you like best.

Remember that much skill can be shown in grouping helping words around the chief words.

Does the second sentence mean the same as the first?

Find different ways of telling what is in each of the other sentences.

In the second sentence find two phrases that tell what life.

Find other words that help to tell what life.

Find a phrase that helps the verb.

Change *the butterfly's* to *of the butterfly*, and then read the sentence.

Make a similar change in the fifth sentence.

Find in how many ways you can arrange the parts of each of these eight sentences.

Tell what kind of sentence each is.

Explain all the punctuation marks.

Additional Lessons.

To the Teacher.—The sentences of this lesson are specially adapted for studying the offices of words and phrases and their **arrangement**.

By easy questions lead the pupils to discover what the different words and phrases do.

Another lesson may be spent in varying and discussing the arrangement.

Get the pupils to change the phraseology and to express each thought in as many ways as possible.

LESSON CII.

Composition.

What to Do.—Make a composition about "The Gay Butterfly." You may change the sentences of the preceding lesson, and work them into your composition. Tell what you think of the butterfly's life as compared with the ant's.

LESSON CIII.

Hints for a Composition.

To the Teacher.—In this and the following lesson let special attention be given to the arrangement. Oral lessons may be needed.

Moths and Butterflies.

Compare the pictures of the moth, on the next page, with those of the butterfly, pages 59 and 63. Which has the more slender body? In which are the three parts more distinct? Which has slender feelers with knobs? Which has curved or fringed feelers? Which rests with

wings held up together? Which, with wings spread out flat, or laid along the back like a cloak? Which has the richer colors? Which flies at twilight or at night? Which is attracted by the lamp? Which is happier in the sunshine? What other differences can you find?

LESSON CIV.

Hints for a Composition.

MOTHS AND BUTTERFLIES—*Continued.*

Six legs—body in three parts—insect—four wings—rolled-up tube, or tongue—thrust into flowers—suck sweet juices—wings covered with beautiful dust—look through a microscope—particles of dust are scales—what you have seen—what you have read or heard about butterflies and moths.

LESSON CV.

Forms of Words Used for Names.

EXERCISE.

1. The dragon-fly catches gnats.
2. A dragon-fly is an insect.

What to See.—The verb tells what something *does* or *is*. *Gnats* here helps *catches* to tell what the dragon-fly does, and *insect* helps *is* to tell what the dragon-fly is.

Which of these words names the things acted upon?

Which names the same thing that the subject names?

Names and words used for names often follow verbs to help in these two ways.

EXERCISE.

1. *I* caught the boy.
2. *We* caught the boy.
3. *He* caught the boy.
4. *She* caught the boy.
5. *They* caught the boy.
6. *Who* caught the boy?
7. It is *I*.
8. It is *we*.
9. It is *he*.
10. It is *she*.
11. It is *they*.
12. It is *who?*

13. The boy caught *me*.
14. The boy caught *us*.
15. The boy caught *him*.
16. The boy caught *her*.
17. The boy caught *them*.
18. *Whom* did the boy catch?

19. The boy ran to *me*.
20. The boy ran from *us*.
21. The boy ran by *him*.
22. The boy ran with *her*.
23. The boy ran around *them*.
24. Around *whom* did the boy run ?

What to See.—Mention in order the subjects in the first six sentences.

Are they names, or words used for names ?

In the next six sentences mention each word that helps the verb to tell or ask who somebody is.

Do these words mean the same as the subjects ?

What two uses have you found for these six words ?

In the next six sentences mention each word that helps *caught* and stands for the name of the one acted upon.

In the last six sentences mention the chief word in each phrase.

What two uses have you found for these six words ?

Do these six words mean the same as the first six words you found ?

See whether you can use *I* and *me* in the same places.

See whether *we* and *us* will exchange places.

I, we, he, she, they, *or* **who** *may be used as the subject, or with the verb to explain the subject.*

Me, us, him, her, them, *or* **whom** *may be used with the verb for the name of the one acted upon, or as the chief word of a phrase.*

To the Teacher.—Let the pupils compare each subject-form with the corresponding object-form. Let them see that the words mean the same, but that they must have different uses.

Let them explain and illustrate the uses of all.

If the teacher wishes to give more drill on the preposition, the preceding lessons afford abundant opportunity.

LESSON CVI.

Forms of Words Used for Names.

EXERCISE.

1. *Whom* do you mean?
2. To *whom* did you speak?
3. Could that boy have been *he?*
4. That person could not have been *she.*
5. For *whom* did he call?
6. Was it *they?*
7. *Who* was there? *I* (*he, she*).
8. *Whom* did she call? *Me* (*us, him, her*).
9. Was it not *I?*
10. Will you go with Kate and *me?*
11. Kate and *I* were there yesterday.

What to See and Do.—Notice that in each sentence we have put a straight line under the subject and a wavy line under the verb.

You may give the uses of the other words, and tell why the words in italics are correct.

Notice that in the seventh example two subjects are underlined, one in the question, and the other in the answer. The words *was there* are understood in the answer.

In the eighth, the words *she called* are understood.

Three answers are suggested in the seventh, and four in the eighth. Give them all separately, first in the short form, then in the full form.

Read these sentences till they seem familiar.

To the Teacher.—The six subject-forms and the six object-forms given on page 185 may be put on the board. The sentences here given may then be dictated with the test words omitted. The pupils may supply the proper words from the lists before them.

Let the pupils supply, in place of the words in italics, all the subject-forms and the object-forms that may be correctly used.

Most pupils will probably need some help in explaining the uses of these case-forms. Give such aid, however, as will leave them to feel that they have done the work themselves.

LESSON CVII.

Forms of Words Used for Names.

EXERCISE.

1. With *whom* are you going?
2. Mary and *I* are going with papa.
3. Papa will take Mary and *me* with him.
4. Between you and *me* this can easily be done.
5. *He* and *I* were beaten.
6. *She* and Fred have called.

7. It makes no difference to either you or *me*.
8. We boys enjoyed it.
9. Who did it? *I* (*we, he, she, they*).
10. To *whom* shall I give it? *Them* (*me, us, him, her*).

What to See and Do.—You will find a straight line under each subject and a wavy line under each verb.

You may tell how each word in italics is used.

For each of these words in italics, tell what word might be used by mistake. Tell why one is right and the other wrong.

Read the ninth and tenth examples and supply the words left out. Supply all the different answers suggested by the words in curves.

Read all the sentences till they seem familiar.

To the Teacher.—See suggestions in the preceding lesson.
Call attention to the order of "Mary and I," "he and I," etc.

LESSON CVIII.

Forms of Words Used for Names.

EXERCISE.

1. I am to blame, not *he*.
2. You must blame me, not *him*.
3. Which is right? *he*, or *I*?
4. You may guess *whom* I saw.
5. You may guess *who* it was.
6. *Whom* did you say he chose?

7. *Who* did you say was chosen?
8. *He* that wins will be rewarded.
9. *Him* that wins I will reward.
10. John is older than *I.*
11. John is as old as *I.*

What to See and Do.—In the first example two sentences are put together. Put in the words left out.

Read the second example, and put in the words left out.

Read the third, and put *is it* before *he,* and the same words again before *I.*

Read the third again, and put *is* before *he,* and *am* before *I.*

Now tell why the italicized words in these three examples are right.

Read the last three words of the fourth, putting *whom* at the end. Why is *whom* correct?

Read the last three words of the fifth, and put *who* at the end. Why is *who* correct?

Read together the first word and the last two words of the sixth, putting *whom* at the end. Why is *whom* correct?

Read together the first word and the last two words of the seventh. Why is *who* correct?

Read the eighth and the ninth, omitting *that wins* from each, and then tell why *he* and *him* are correct.

Read the tenth and put *am* at the end. Why is *I* correct?

Explain the eleventh in the same way.

In place of *I,* in the tenth, put *we, he, she, they,* and *who.* Make similar changes in the eleventh.

Explain all.

To the Teacher.—In these hints we have tried to confine the pupils' attention to the clause containing the word in question. Let them see that the other clause has nothing to do with the form of this word.

Pupils can generally detect such errors when the sentence or clause is read in its "natural" order.

The pupils may read these hints and questions in the class, and discuss them freely. With the aid that has been given, we believe very little assistance will be needed from the teacher.

Additional Lessons.

Sentences illustrating the uses of these subject-forms and object-forms should be varied in every possible way, and dictated as suggested before.

Let no time be wasted on those constructions in which pupils are not liable to err.

LESSON CIX.

Connecting Words—Comma.

EXERCISE.

1. Anna, Lucy, and Jane are going.
2. Anna, Lucy, or Jane is going.
3. Neither Anna, Lucy, nor Jane is going.
4. Neither the fly, the butterfly, nor the grasshopper lays up food.
5. A red, white, and blue flag was flying.
6. A red, a white, and a blue flag were flying.
7. The first, second, and third verses were read.
8. The first, the second, and the third verse were read.

What to See.—In the first sentence what words are used in the same way?

What connects these words?

Where is the connecting word understood?

What have you learned about the comma as here used?

In the first sentence how many are said to be going?

In the second, is one, or are three, said to be going?

In the third, are the persons named as taken together, or separately?

In the fourth, are the three insects named as taken together, or separately?

What difference do you here find between *and* and *or* or *nor*?

Show that *are, is,* and *lays* are correctly used.

How are the helping words connected in the fifth?

In the sixth, the word *flag* is understood after *red* and after *white.* This we know because *a* is used three times.

How are the helping words connected in the seventh?

In the eighth, the word *verse* is understood after *first* and after *second.* We know that each *the* requires a name.

Explain the use of the commas.

With neither *use* nor, *not* or.

What to Do.—Write five sentences using *neither* and *nor.*

Additional Lesson.

To the Teacher.—A lesson on the correct use of *a* or *an* and *the,* with connected terms, is here suggested.

Let the pupils see that to repeat *the* in the seventh sentence would be wrong, as *verses* would be understood with *first* and *second*. Let them see that to use only the first *the* in the eighth sentence would be wrong, as *verse* names one thing, and the same thing can not be first, second, and third.

Guard them against such common errors as, " Read the fourth, fifth, and sixth stanza ; " " Read the fourth, the fifth, and the sixth stanzas."

If this is found too difficult here, let it be deferred for a review.

LESSON CX.
Connecting Words — Comma.
EXERCISE.

1. Harry kept his eyes open. He saw many curious things.

2. The grasshopper can travel by long leaps. He can sail through the air on wings.

3. The grasshopper can not walk well on the level. He can climb.

4. Many wonderful things can be seen only through a microscope. They are very small.

5. Touch the moth's wings. Your hand is covered with powder.

6. The moth can drink from the flowers' deep cups. It carries a long tube rolled up.

7. The moth visits the flowers. The sun has gone down.

8. Insects have little holes along their sides. Through these holes they breathe.

9. This is the girl. You saw her yesterday.

What to Do.—Join the two sentences in each of the groups above, using these **Connecting Words :**—

and, or, but, because, if, for, when, which, that.

In the eighth group join the sentences by changing *these holes* to *which.*

In the ninth, join the sentences by changing *her,* first to *that* and then to *whom.* No comma will be needed.

In each of your other new sentences put a comma before the connecting word.

A comma is generally used between two sentences that are joined, but sometimes such sentences read together so closely that no comma is needed.

Be careful not to join sentences that do not belong together. You would not say, "Harry is a good boy, *and* his father is a farmer."

Write sentences, and join them.

LESSON CXI.

Hints for a Composition.

To the Teacher.—Let special attention be given to connectives and to arrangement. An oral lesson may be profitable.

The Grasshopper.

Body in three parts—six legs and four wings on the middle part—wide collar—upper wings, or wing-covers, long, straight—under wings, delicate, fold like a fan, tuck under covers, fine dress coat under plain overcoat—front legs short—hind legs very long—does not walk much on the level—can climb up a stem—strong thigh—sharp points below—famous

jumper—length of leap—eats leaves and grass, or animal food—other things that you know, or that you can find out from the picture.

LESSON CXII.
A Study of Sentences.

To the Teacher.—Let special attention be given to arrangement and variety. The teacher must determine how much of the work should be written.

1. In Mr. Grasshopper's wing is a drumhead stretched tight.

2. By moving one wing-cover over the other he makes his cheerful, chirping music for the amusement of Mrs. Grasshopper.

3. Locusts are very often called grasshoppers.

4. Mr. Locust makes music by rubbing his rough hind legs over the ridges on his wings.

5. The grasshopper's shrill music brings to us cheerful thoughts of pleasant summer days.

6. This "green little vaulter in the sunny grass" dances and sings merrily through one happy summer, but dies on the approach of winter.

What to See and Do.—Find the two chief words in the first sentence.

What phrase helps *is* by telling where the drumhead is?

What does the expression *stretched tight* describe?

Begin this sentence with *there is*, and find the best way of arranging it.

Find the two chief words in the second sentence.

What word helps *makes* by telling what he makes, or by naming the thing acted upon?

What phrase tells how he makes music?

For the amusement of Mrs. Grasshopper does what?

Find another way of arranging this sentence.

Omit *he*, change *makes* to *is made*, and then find different ways of arranging the sentence.

Find the subject and the verb in the third sentence.

When are locusts called grasshoppers?

What helping word is joined to another helping word?

What name helps *are called* and explains the subject?
What other positions can *very often* take?
Which sounds the best?

Arrange the other three sentences in as many ways as possible, and tell which way you like best.

In the fourth sentence change *Mr. Locust* to a possessive, *makes* to *is made,* and then arrange the sentence.

In the fifth, put in *by,* change *brings* to *are brought,* and then arrange the sentence in different ways.

In the sixth, are some words taken from the poet, Leigh Hunt.

How are they marked?

Does the first word of this quotation begin with a capital? Why? (See pages 126 and 127.)

Is it separated from the other words by commas? Why?

Additional Lessons.

To the Teacher.—The questions on the first three sentences, to bring out what the different words and phrases do, will suggest similar questions for the remaining sentences. (See "To the Teacher," at the end of Lesson CI.)

LESSON CXIII.

Hints for a Composition.

THE GRASSHOPPER.

What to Do.—Make a composition about "The Grasshopper." Say, if you wish, the same things that are said about him in the preceding lesson, but say these things in your own language. You must add what is necessary to make a connected story, or composition.

LESSON CXIV.

Direct and Indirect Quotations.

EXERCISE.

1. The fox said, " The grapes are sour."
2. The fox said that the grapes were sour.
3. " Can the owl sing ? " asked Dick.
4. Dick asked whether the owl could sing.

What to See.—Find all the differences between the first and the second sentence. (See pages 124 and 127.)

Find all the differences between the third and the fourth.

When we tell what some one has said, and use his exact words, we make a **Direct Quotation.**

When we tell what some one has said, but do not use his exact words, we make an **Indirect Quotation.**

Which are the indirect quotations in this " exercise " ?

Is the indirect quotation inclosed within quotation marks ?

Does it begin with a capital ?

Is it separated from the other words by a comma ?

Give all the differences between a direct quotation and an indirect quotation.

In the third sentence the question mark separates the quotation from the other words, so no comma is needed.

Notice that the direct quotation in the third sentence is also a **Direct Question.**

What words tell what Dick asked, without giving his exact language?

These words make an **Indirect Question.**

Is the indirect question followed by a question mark?

On page 125 find a quotation that does not begin with a capital, and that is not separated from the other words by commas.

Tell why this quotation is so written. (See page 126, near the bottom.)

What to Do.—Change the first sentence, and put the quotation at the beginning.

Change the third, and put the quotation at the end.

Do not omit the commas.

Write two sentences containing direct quotations, and then make the quotations indirect.

Let one of the quotations be a question.

Write sentences, using the following sayings as direct, and as indirect, quotations:—

Politeness costs nothing.
There is no place like home.

To the Teacher.—In converting direct conversation into indirect, it is often very difficult to avoid confusion in the use of *he, him, she, her,* etc. The following selections were made as offering the least difficulty.

Short selections from dialogues, found in the Reader or elsewhere, may be changed into the indirect form to show the pupils the necessity of great caution in the use of pronouns.

LESSON CXV.

Quotations.

THE HUNTER AND THE WOODCUTTER.

Copy the following, and notice everything carefully :—

"Have you seen any tracks of a lion?" asked a boastful hunter of a woodcutter whom he met.

"Oh," said the woodcutter, "I can show you the lion himself."

Then the hunter was pale with fright, his teeth chattered, and he said, "I want to see his tracks only; I don't want to see the lion."

There are those who are brave with words only, and not with deeds.

What to See.—Does the writer of this story use the hunter's and the woodcutter's exact words?

Find here a direct question quoted.

What changes must be made when this becomes an indirect question?

Which quotation is divided by three of the story-writer's own words?

Explain the quotation marks. (See page 130.)

What do the two commas here mark off?

What to Do.—Write this story and make the direct quotations indirect.

Tell in your own language what the story teaches.

LESSON CXVI.

Quotations.

THE SENSIBLE WILD BOAR—A FABLE.

Copy the following, and notice everything carefully:—

A fox one day found a wild boar sharpening his tusks on the trunk of a tree.

"Why do you whet your tusks now?" said the fox. "There is no sign of the coming of the hunter or the hounds."

"My dear friend," said the wild boar, "it would never do for me to be sharpening my weapons when I ought to be using them."

Learn to be in time.

What to See.—Find here a quotation that is made up of a direct question and a statement.

Are the words that divide this quotation marked off by commas? Why?

How can this quotation be made indirect?

What to Do.—Write this fable and make the quotations indirect.

Tell in your own language what the fable teaches.

To the Teacher.—The use of the single quotation marks to inclose a quotation within a quotation may be explained in a review, or when met in copying.

LESSON CXVII.

Review of Capitals.

To the Teacher.—We do not offer the following as formal rules. We should not hold the pupils to an exact repetition of the language here given.

Every Sentence *should begin with a capital letter.*

When a direct quotation makes complete sense, it begins with a capital.

The words I *and* O *should be written in capitals.*

Particular Names *begin with capitals.*

Two or more names forming one particular name should each begin with a capital; as, *James Russell Lowell.*

In such names as *Gulf of Mexico, Cape of Good Hope,* of does not begin with a capital.

In the title of a book or the subject of a composition the first word and the principal words begin with capitals; as, *Everything in its Right Place.*

The names of the days of the week and the months of the year begin with capitals.

All names of God begin with capitals; as, "The *Lord* rules."

Words made from particular names begin with capitals; as, "We study the *English* language."

The first word of every line of poetry begins with a capital; as,—

> The Autumn is old;
> The sear leaves are flying;
> He hath gathered up gold,
> And now he is dying.
>
> —*Hood.*

EXERCISE.

1. Shall I lend you Hans Christian Andersen's "Tales for Children"?
2. Have you read George MacDonald's "At the Back of the North Wind"?
3. Frank asked, "Does the water of Lake Superior flow into the Gulf of St. Lawrence?"
4. Your Heavenly Father feedeth them.
5. Columbus sailed Friday, August 3, 1492.

What to See and Do.—Copy these five examples, and explain the use of each capital.

What titles of books are here quoted?

In the first example, is the quotation a part of the question? Is it in the second? Notice that the quotation marks are within the question mark.

In the third example we quote the question, and so the question mark is within the quotation marks.

To the Teacher.—Only your more observing pupils will fully understand the relation of the quotation marks to the question mark till the matter is brought up for review. Similar relations between the exclamation mark and the quotation marks may then be explained.

In a review, it may be well to show that the third sentence is a statement, and that, although the question mark belongs only to the quotation, the period is omitted. The omission of the period after the exclamation mark may also be illustrated.

LESSON CXVIII.

Review of Capitals.

What to Do.—Write sentences that will show what you have learned about capitals.

LESSON CXIX.

Review of Punctuation.

To the Teacher.—See "To the Teacher," Lesson CXVII.

A **Period** *is placed at the end of a statement or a command.*
A **Period** *is placed after an abbreviation or initial.*
A **Question Mark** *is placed after a direct question.*
An **Exclamation Mark** *is placed after an exclamation.*
A *direct quotation is inclosed within* **Quotation Marks.**
The name of the one addressed is separated from the rest of the sentence by a **Comma** *or by two commas.*
Words or phrases connected and used in the same way are separated by **Commas** *unless all the connecting words are put in.*

Use the **Comma** *where there is a slight break between words, or where the sentence should be divided to help the reader.*

What to Do.—Write sentences showing the uses of the period.

Write sentences showing the use of the question mark, the exclamation mark, and the quotation marks.

EXERCISE.

1. Ants, bees, and wasps are busy creatures.
2. Ants and bees and wasps are busy creatures.
3. Brave, manly deeds will be remembered.
4. Brave and manly deeds will be remembered.
5. Two happy little birds are singing together.
6. The ant, certainly, is not lazy.
7. Ants and bees, with their little brains, do much thinking.
8. John, the gardener, gave us some roses.
9. We girls are fond of roses.
10. Insects have six legs, but spiders have eight.
11. We shall not go if it rains.

What to See.—In each of the first four sentences tell what words are connected and used in the same way.

Tell the differences between the first and second sentences, and between the third and fourth.

When three or more words or phrases are connected, the connecting word is generally put between the last two only, as in the first sentence.

When the connecting words are all used, the commas are not needed.

What does the comma in the third sentence take the place of?

Could a connecting word be used between *two* and *happy*, or between *happy* and *little*?

Is the comma needed?

Notice that in the sixth sentence *certainly* does not read closely with the other words. There is a break or pause before it, and another after it.

In the seventh, what phrase does not read closely with the other words?

In the eighth, *the gardener* explains *John*, and makes a slight break.

In the ninth, *girls* explains *we*, but it reads so closely with the other words that no comma is needed.

Do the parts of the last two sentences read together closely?

Explain the use of all the commas.

Find other examples similar to the first, third, sixth, seventh, eighth, tenth, and eleventh.

To the Teacher.—Pupils of the primary grades will need to use few marks other than the terminal marks and the comma.

In copying selections, and in reading, the semicolon may be noticed as indicating a wider separation than the comma.

The dash may also be noticed as marking a sudden break.

When a quotation preceded by a colon is met, let the pupils see that the quotation is more formally presented, and that a longer pause is required.

LESSON CXX.

Review of Punctuation.

What to Do.—Write sentences to show what you have learned about the comma.

Explain the use of the comma in the script sentences on pages 103, 104, and 107.

Tell why the comma is used or is not used, with the helping words in Lesson XC.

LESSON CXXI.

A Study of Sentences — Composition.

THE BUTTERFLY'S BABY.

EXERCISE.

1. The butterfly sips sweet juices from the flowers' delicate cups.
2. Her greedy baby will devour green leaves.
3. How does she know this?
4. She always fastens her eggs to the right plant.
5. In a week or two, out comes baby caterpillar.
6. How it does eat and grow!
7. Then it ties itself fast with silk from its mouth, and sleeps.

What to Do.—Explain the mark at the end of each sentence.

Explain the use of (') and *s* in *flowers'*.
Find the chief parts of each sentence.
Change these sentences into your own language, and make of them a connected story.

LESSON CXXII.

A Study of Sentences — Composition.

WONDERFUL THINGS HAPPEN—THE BUTTERFLY.

EXERCISE.

1. The insect's whole body is now made over.
2. Finally the little gray case stirs and breaks.
3. Two bright eyes look out on this queer world.
4. The whole body is dragged out.
5. The closely folded wings open little by little and harden in the sun.
6. Oh, what a glorious creature!
7. Away it soars among the sunbeams.
8. Have you ever seen a cocoon or chrysalis open?

What to Do.—Find the chief parts of the sentences above.
Which group of words has no verb?
Change the language above into your own, and make a connected story.

To the Teacher.—Pupils may be exercised in finding the helping words in the two preceding lessons.
Both oral and written composition lessons are here suggested.

LESSON CXXIII.

Hints for a Composition.

THE DRAGON-FLY.

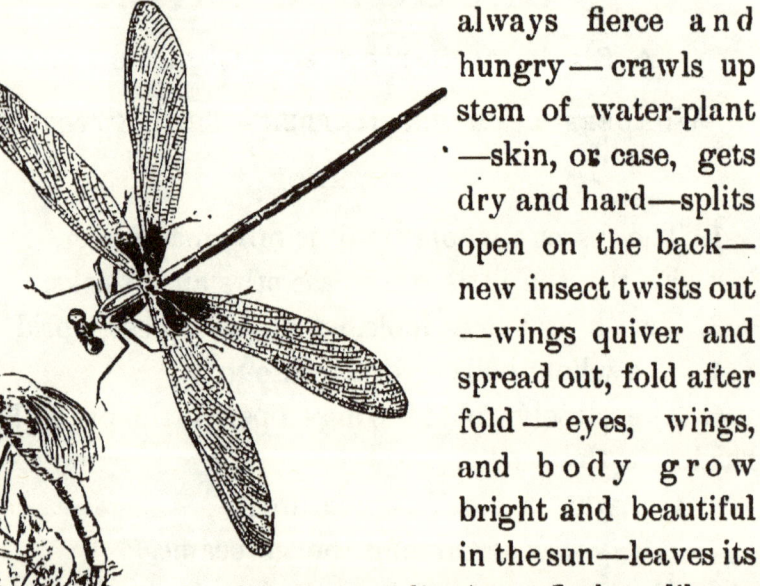

Curious creature in the water—six legs—no wings—always fierce and hungry—crawls up stem of water-plant—skin, or case, gets dry and hard—splits open on the back—new insect twists out—wings quiver and spread out, fold after fold—eyes, wings, and body grow bright and beautiful in the sun—leaves its old shape clinging—flashes like a streak of light back and forth over the pond—hungrier than ever—eats mosquitoes and other insects—no sting—harmless—four large, lace-like wings with rainbow colors—eyes like flaming jewels—beautiful in color, shape, and motion.

What to Do.—These broken sentences will help you to write about "The Dragon-fly."

LESSON CXXIV.

The Verb — Review.

EXERCISE.

1. On one side *are* trees.
2. Of words there *is* no lack.
3. How many legs *has* each of these insects?
4. Not one in twenty *comes* back.
5. There *are* only ashes left.
6. Neither of you *has* guessed it.
7. Near the mill *stand* some old poplar trees.
8. Every one of these words *was* used.
9. Not one out of ten persons *uses* this word right.
10. Of what use *are* study and books?
11. Two weeks' vacation *is* not enough.
12. Three hours' rest *was* taken.
13. There *are* Jack Wren and Jenny Wren.
14. Here *is* Jack Wren and Jenny Wren's nest.

What to See and Do.—Notice the straight line under each subject and the wavy line under each verb.

Read each sentence and put the subject before its verb.

Which sentences sound better with the subject after the verb?

Show that each word in italics is correct.

Write sentences beginning with *there is, there are, here is,* and *here are.*

To the Teacher.—Let the singular and the plural form of each verb in the "exercise" be put on the board; then dictate the sentences, leaving the pupils to supply the test words from the list on the board.

Let the pupils see that "*Jack Wren* and *Jenny Wren's* nest" shows that both have the same nest, and that "*Jack Wren's* and *Jenny Wren's* nest" shows that each has a separate nest. So with "*Smith* and *Brown's* store," and "*Smith's* and *Brown's* store." In primary teaching it is sometimes better to bring in such instruction incidentally, anticipating a fuller discussion in the grammar classes.

LESSON CXXV.

Using the Right Verb.

EXERCISE.

1. I *shall* probably go to-morrow.
2. I *shall* be glad to see you.
3. I *will* get it for you.
4. *Shall* I go?
5. *May* I read it? You *may*.
6. *Can* I read it? You *can* if you will try.
7. *May* I speak to you? You *may*.
8. Will you *teach* me to do it?
9. Who *taught* you to do it?
10. You *ought* not to do it.

What to See.—Read these sentences and notice the use of the words in italics.

In the first and the second sentence the speaker simply tells what will happen in the future.

It would be wrong to use *will* with *I* in such sentences.

In the third sentence the speaker promises.

"**Will I?**" *is not used;* for a person does not ask others whether he himself is willing.

In the fifth and the seventh sentence *may* is used to ask, and to give, permission.

It would be wrong to use **can** *to ask, or give, permission.*

In the sixth, the speaker asks whether he is able.

It would be wrong to use **learn** *for* **teach** in the eighth sentence, *or* **learnt** *for* **taught** in the ninth.

It is wrong to use **had** *or* **hadn't** *before* **ought**.

What to Do.—Make sentences showing the right use of the words in italics.

To the Teacher.—Find, by oral or written exercises, which of these words your pupils use incorrectly, and drill accordingly.

LESSON CXXVI.
Arranging and Joining Sentences.

To the Teacher.—An oral lesson should precede the written.

An Old Man's Story.

We sailed toward the west. We bade good-by to friends. We left our homes. Our ships cut through the waves. They bore us rapidly over the water. The wind blew steadily from the east. The breeze did not change. We blessed the breeze. Our hearts were full of hope.

Bidding good-by to friends, we left our homes, and

sailed toward the west. With the wind blowing steadily from the east, our ships cut through the waves, and bore us rapidly over the water. Our hearts were full of hope, and we blessed the breeze that did not change.

What to See.—Notice that these sentences as first written are not properly arranged.

If we should put them in the right order, and make no other change, our story would still be "jerky."

Find how they are put together in the second group.

Which are changed to phrases?

Which are linked together by connecting words?

Do you like this arrangement better? Why?

What to Do.—You may continue this story by putting together properly the sentences in the next two paragraphs.

Remember that there is danger of using too many ands, or other connecting words, and of joining sentences that should be separate.

On we sped. The third and fourth weeks passed. All was sea. Two weeks were gone. No land appeared. Our men grew gloomy. They were once so bold and full of hope. "When shall we see our homes again?"

One night thick clouds hung over the sea. A fierce storm burst upon us. The waves rose. The wind came in gusts. We drove before the storm. We drove for three days and nights. Then the rain fell. The wind ceased.

To the Teacher.—In these lessons let the oral exercises, as far as possible, be reviews.

The punctuation of the paragraph in italics may be noticed. In the next paragraph attention may be called to the correct and incorrect ways of writing "the third and fourth weeks" (see pages 191, 192), to making the direct quotation indirect, etc.

In rearranging and joining the sentences, get from the pupils a variety of forms.

LESSON CXXVII.

Arranging and Joining Sentences.

AN OLD MAN'S STORY—*Continued.*

To the Teacher.—An oral lesson should precede the written.

One of our men pointed to a bird. It was flying slowly overhead. One day I heard a shout. I had never seen so welcome a sight. The bird must have come from land. The land could not be far distant. I knew that.

One day I heard a shout, and one of our men pointed to a bird flying slowly overhead. I had never seen so welcome a sight; for I knew that the bird must have come from land, and that the land could not be far distant.

What to See.—Find how the sentences of the first group are put together in the second.

Tell why the second arrangement is better.

What to Do.—Continue the story by putting together properly the sentences in the next two paragraphs.

We saw no land. Three days passed. There were now many signs of it. Weeds floated on the waves. Birds were on the wing.

We watched till the dawn. That night we stood on the deck. We saw a long, gray line of coast. It was like a cloud on the edge of the sea. With what shouts that sight was greeted! With what cheers!

LESSON CXXVIII.

Arranging and Joining Sentences.

To the Teacher.—An oral lesson should precede the written.

AN OLD MAN'S STORY—*Continued.*

We rowed through the calm waves. We left the ship in our boats. We leaped on shore. We kissed the earth. We kneeled down.

We left the ship in our boats; and, rowing through the calm waves, we leaped on shore, and kneeling down, kissed the earth.

What to See.—Tell how the sentences of the first group are put together in the second.

What to Do.—Continue the story by putting together the sentences in the next two paragraphs, and then add what you wish.

The men soon came round us. They dwelt in the New World. Their skins were dark. They led us to a large hut. They found that we did not mean to hurt or wrong them. The hut was not far from the beach. They gave us this as our house for the night.

Nets made of reeds hung from the walls and roof. The hut was built of boughs, canes, and trunks of trees. We lay down in these nets. We slept through the night peacefully.

Such was the story of ———, who left ———.

LESSON CXXIX.

Hints for a Composition.

THE FROG.

Which legs are short? Describe the hind legs. Which toes are webbed? Is the frog a great leaper and swimmer? Why? Which toes turn in? Which turn out? What more can you learn from the picture?

Glossy green coat — light vest and trousers — dives into mud — always clean — cold weather — no feathers, fur, nor wool — goes to bed in the mud — bottom of pond—sleeps all winter—cozy as if under blankets—early in spring—sings bass—frog concerts every evening—sits for hours basking in sun—what you have seen or heard.

What to Do.—Let these "hints" help you to make a composition about "The Frog."

Be careful not to make your sentences too long or too short. Group them into paragraphs.

LESSON CXXX.
Hints for a Composition.

THE TOAD.

Rough, warty back—frog smooth—toad's hind legs shorter—not so much web—lives on land—baby frog and baby toad in water (*tadpoles*)—frog likes sunshine—toad seeks shade—scratches hole to sit in—out at night—hunts insects and worms—gardener's friend—curious tongue like frog—fast to front part of jaw—free end turned back into mouth—tip sticky—darts out—touches insect—has him—worm twice as long as himself—with little hands crams in wriggling worm bit by bit—all in—big mouth closes with snap—blinking eyes—how good!—cold weather—goes to sleep—hole in the ground.

What to Do.—Use these "hints" to help in making a composition about "The Toad."

LESSON CXXXI.

A Study of Sentences.

1. Washington, with his defeated army, was in the city of New York, just after the battle of Long Island.
2. By crossing the East River the British might entrap his whole army.
3. Some brave, cool-headed man must enter the enemy's camp and learn his plans.
4. Captain Nathan Hale, a brilliant and handsome young man, came forward and said, "I will undertake it."
5. On his way back to Washington's camp Captain Hale was captured, and, soon after, was hanged.
6. His last words were, "I only regret that I have but one life to lose for my country."

What to See and Do.—Copy the fourth and the sixth sentence.

Find the chief words in the other sentences.

Explain the capitals and punctuation in all the sentences.

Find what changes you can make in these sentences without changing the meaning.

To the Teacher.—By the aid of easy questions, pupils may, perhaps, point out the chief parts of connected clauses and note how they are joined.

LESSON CXXXII.

Composition.

A HERO OF THE REVOLUTION.

What to Do.—Write a composition, taking for your subject "A Hero of the Revolution." You may get the facts for your story from the preceding lesson, or elsewhere; but use your own language.

LESSON CXXXIII.

Hints for a Composition—Quotations.

THE TORTOISE AND THE HARE—A FABLE.

Hare made fun of tortoise—said tortoise had slow way, creeping along—tortoise asked hare to race—hare said tortoise was in fun—agreed to race—asked fox to mark bounds and give prize—fox showed where to start, how far to run—tortoise lost no time—started promptly—jogged straight on—hare sure he could win—lay down—took nap—awoke—ran fast—came to end—tortoise already there—what we learn from this.

What to Do.—Write this fable as if you were using the exact words of the hare and the tortoise.
Get up a lively conversation between the animals.
Be careful to use quotation marks correctly.

LESSON CXXXIV.

Hints for a Composition — Quotations.

Trying to Please Everybody.

Man and son driving donkey to the fair—met troop of girls, talking, laughing—one cried out—ever see such fools—trudge on foot—might ride—man put son on donkey—group of old men—one said—respect to old age these days—idle young rogue riding—father has to walk—son got down—man took his place—company of women and children—several tongues at once—lazy old fellow—ride—poor little boy—hardly keep up—man took boy up behind.

What to Do.—Tell this story, using the exact language of the different persons. Use quotation marks carefully.

LESSON CXXXV.

Hints for a Composition — Quotations.

Trying to Please Everybody—*Continued.*

Almost reached town—townsman asked whether donkey belonged to man—yes—should have thought not—load him so heavily—two were better able to carry poor beast—man willing to do anything to please—could try—tied donkey's legs together—stout pole—tried to carry him on shoulders—crowds ran—laughed—bridge—donkey kicked—tumbled off pole—drowned—man and son went home—tried to please everybody—pleased nobody—lost donkey.

What to Do.—Use these "hints" to finish the story you began in the preceding lesson. Use quotations.

LESSON CXXXVI.

Hints for a Composition.

The Wasp—A Mason.

Insect—slender body—three parts—six legs—two feelers—four thin wings—wings at rest lie close to sides—

what you may see in the picture—one kind a mason—brought mud in balls—clay hut—closed door and flew away—broke in—found baby—bodies of spiders and flies—put into deep sleep by sting—baby hungry, find plenty of food—baby, first an egg—then little, soft worm (*larva*)—spins silken cover around itself—sleeps (*pupa*)—legs and wings grow—throws off clothes—breaks out of house—full grown wasp.

What to Do.—From the "hints" here given, and from what you know about mud wasps, make a composition.

LESSON CXXXVII.

Hints for a Composition.

THE WASP—A PAPERMAKER.

One kind a papermaker before man learned—piece of old wood—scrapes off bits like thread—wets with glue from mouth—rolls into a ball—flies home—spreads ball out thin—uses 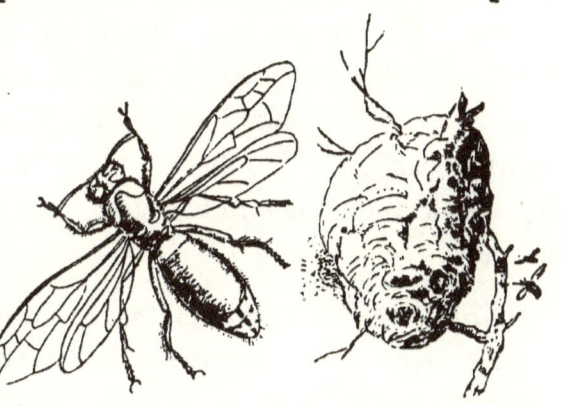 tongue, jaws, and feet—flat feet on hind legs help to lay down paper—little paper rooms with six sides like bees' cells—one room for each baby—makes wax—puts wax lids on cells—makes varnish to keep cells dry—some hang nests in trees—round or shape of top—hornet, kind of wasp.

What to Do.—Write a composition about these little papermakers.

LESSON CXXXVIII.

Arranging and Joining Sentences.

A Brave Boy.

A little boy and his sister were playing. The shouts of some men alarmed them. A mad dog was rushing toward them. The boy took off his jacket. He wrapped it around his arm. He boldly held out the covered limb. The dog seized the arm and kept worrying at it. The men came up and killed the animal. The boy was not injured. The dog's teeth could not penetrate the thick folds. One of the men asked the boy why he did not run away. The man said that the boy could have escaped easily. The brave little fellow said that the dog would have bitten his sister. He said that she could not run.

What to Do.—These sentences seem rather bare, and when we read them together, the story hitches along unpleasantly.

You have learned how to finish such sentences, and how to join them in various ways.

The first sentence, for instance, does not tell *when* or *where* the children were playing. Such little incidents are left for you to fill in.

Tell the story just as you think it happened.

In telling what the man and the boy said, give their exact words, that is, make direct quotations.

LESSON CXXXIX.

Hints for a Composition.

THE DANDELION—A FABLE.

Dandelion did its best—bright and gay all day—happy, broad, golden face not admired—wonder why nobody likes me—sadly—other flowers better than I—anybody ever care about me—shall I shut leaves and die—no, no, —said gentle wind—passed over—keep on hoping—just then large bee buzzing—long meadow grass—rested on dandelion—honey in its heart—beautiful flower—glad— found you—golden face to sun—I have not lived for nothing—each of us can do some good to somebody.

What to Do.—Tell this fable, and make it as bright and interesting as possible.

Represent the dandelion, the wind, and the bee as talking, and use their exact words, as you imagine them.

Be careful to put in the quotation marks, commas, and other marks that are here omitted.

How many denying words in "I have not lived for nothing"?

Compare this with "I have not lived for anything," "I have lived for nothing," and "I have lived for something."

What mistakes are sometimes made with such words?

LESSON CXL.

Hints for a Composition.

BRUCE AND THE SPIDER.

King Robert Bruce of Scotland had fled from his country—hiding in hut—island—coast of Ireland—lost all castles but one—left queen in this—castle fell into hands of English—Bruce in great despair—on wretched bed—gave up all hope—looking up—spider trying to swing from one beam to another to fasten web—failed, again and again—six vain attempts—king interested—six times have I been defeated—if spider succeeds next time, I will try again—spider succeeded—Bruce followed its example—persevering spider—successful king.

What to Do.—Tell the story of "Bruce and the Spider" in your own words.

In telling what Bruce said to himself use *indirect* quotations, that is, do not use his exact words. Remember that no quotation marks will then be needed.

LESSON CXLI.

Hints for a Composition.

THE CRICKET.

Jolly little fellow—short, thick body—black and brown—shiny black head—front wings, thick for covers

—under wings fold lengthwise—hind legs strong—great leaper—feelers longer than body—Mr. Cricket's music all night—please Mrs. Cricket—music in late summer and autumn—left wing-cover is the bow, right is the fiddle—lives alone—field-cricket—hole in the ground—eats vegeta-

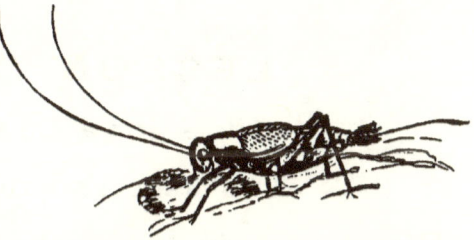

bles, animal food, woolen clothes, almost anything—Dickens's "Cricket on the Hearth"—what you know about crickets.

What to Do.—Get what hints you can from these broken sentences, and make a composition about "Crickets."

LESSON CXLII.

Hints for a Composition.

TWO REAL FRIENDS.

South of Italy—beautiful island—Sicily—was built famous city of Syracuse—ruler of Syracuse, cruel tyrant—condemned Pythias to death—privilege of going home, seeing family, and arranging affairs—king's condition was, a friend should take the place of Pythias—king, selfish himself, thought no friend could be found—a dear and true friend, Damon, came forward and offered himself—king surprised—Pythias visited home—started to return—met wild beasts—attacked by robbers—flood—broken bridges.

What to Do.—Tell this story as you think it happened.

LESSON CXLIII.
Hints for a Composition.
Two Real Friends—*Continued.*

King visited Damon in prison—your friend will not return—if possible, O King—I have no family—love friend—easy to die for him—fatal day—Damon on scaffold—crowd looked on, hardly breathing—sound of hoofs—horse covered with foam, galloping—it is he—it is Pythias—a loud shout—off his horse, on the scaffold, in the arms of Damon—my friend, Damon—do your duty, executioner—king in amazement—no—let faithful friend live—me, if worthy, third in this bond of friendship.

What to Do.—Finish the story, making it as strong and as real as possible.

You will need some exclamation marks.

LESSON CXLIV.
Hints for a Composition.
A Noble Revenge.

Officer struck a private—soldier flushed—would make him repent it—same day—fierce battle—enemy carried off flag—volunteers to recover it—a private soldier led—a few men followed—a gallant attack—desperate fight—came back with the torn and blackened flag—an officer met them—found the leader—the private soldier whom he had struck—officer begged to be forgiven—told you—make you repent it.

What to Do.—Tell this story as you think it happened.

LESSON CXLV.

Hints for a Composition.

THE LITTLE BOATMAN.

Little insect—two wings—sits on leaf—water—fastens eggs together—makes boat of eggs—hatch in few days—lively little creatures in the water—wrigglers—grown in few weeks—come to top of water—sunny day—skin dries—little canoe—splits open—mosquito's head—draws himself out—stands in his boat—wings dry in sun—flies away—many drown getting out—food for fishes—others, food for birds, dragon-flies, etc.—what you know about mosquitoes.

What to Do.—Write the story of this very queer little boatman.

LESSON CXLVI.

Hints for a Composition.

To the Teacher.—An oral lesson is here suggested. The sentences may be studied as to their parts. Pupils may state the facts in their own language.

A Roman Hero.

1. In a war between the Romans and the people of Carthage, Regulus fell into the hands of the enemy.

2. After a long time his captors sent him, with some of their own men, to Rome to ask for peace.

3. Before starting he made a promise to return.

4. The message sent by his masters was given to the Romans.

5. By advising peace or by breaking his promise, Regulus could have saved his life.

6. The captive warrior kept his promise, and returned to torture and death.

What to Do.—Tell the story of Regulus in your own language.

LESSON CXLVII.

Letter-Writing.

Kinds of Note-paper.—The three chief sizes of note-paper are known as *commercial,* *octavo,* and *billet.*

The commercial size, the largest, is for long letters or for men's use generally; the octavo, for short letters and ordinary notes; and the billet, for invitations and answers to invitations.

Unruled white paper of medium thickness and good quality is preferred.

Folding and Envelopes.—Commercial note-paper is generally folded twice—first from the bottom, then from the top—so as to divide the length of the page into three parts nearly equal.

The envelope should be just large enough to receive easily the sheet thus folded.

The smaller sizes of note-paper are usually folded but once—evenly from bottom to top—to fit envelopes nearly square.

Envelopes should be of the same color and quality as the paper.

Letter-sheets.—Letter-sheets of different sizes are used for business purposes. They are generally made to fit the envelopes by folding once from bottom to top, and twice the other way, dividing the width of the sheet into three parts nearly equal.

Margins.—On the left of each page there should be a margin about half an inch wide, varying with the size of the paper; and, on the right, the edge should not be crowded nor the lines uneven.

A margin of at least an inch should be left at the top of the first page. If the letter or note occupies but a few lines of one page, it should begin farther down.

Ink.—Use black ink.

General Directions.—Keep your lines straight, with equal distances between.

Do not blot your paper, or soil it with your fingers. Press in all folds evenly.

To the Teacher.—This lesson may be read and discussed in the class. An object lesson may follow, illustrating the different sizes of paper and envelopes, and the methods of folding.

Pupils may make on their slates outlines of note-sheets and envelopes, indicating margins, lines, and paragraphs. The margin left in beginning a paragraph should be twice the width of the margin for other lines.

The following average sizes may aid in the object lesson or the slate work:—

Commercial note, $7\frac{7}{8} \times 4\frac{7}{8}$ inches; envelope, $5\frac{1}{8} \times 3\frac{1}{8}$ inches. Octavo, $7 \times 4\frac{1}{2}$ inches; envelope, $4\frac{5}{8} \times 3\frac{3}{4}$ inches. Billet, $6\frac{1}{8} \times 4$ inches; envelope, $4\frac{1}{4} \times 3\frac{1}{4}$ inches.

LESSON CXLVIII.
Letter-Writing.

From the following form, learn to name the parts of a letter :—

[Heading.]
*Saginaw, Mich.,
June 10, 1891.*

[Salutation.]
Dear Uncle Rufus,

[Body of the Letter.] ——————

————————————————————

————————

[Complimentary Close.]
Your affectionate nephew,

[Signature.]
Edgar J. Peck.

[Address.]
*Rufus Roe, Esq.,
Tacoma, Wash.*

[Superscription.]   STAMP

*Rufus Roe, Esq.,
Tacoma,
Wash.*

What to Do.—You may use the form above and write Edgar's letter.

Tell about a serious accident that happened to his father and mother when they were driving.

LESSON CXLIX.

Letter-Writing.

Dear Clara,

_____

_____

Affectionately yours,
Anna Irving.

Bismarck, N. Dak.,
Tuesday, Sep. 9, '92.

What to See.—Describe the letter-form above.

Notice that the "heading" and the "address" are omitted.

What takes the place of the "heading"?

What to Do.—Write Anna's letter.

Begin by telling when Clara's letter was received, and then tell briefly what happened during the week past.

LESSON CL.

Business Letter.

Sundance, Crook Co., Wyo.,
Nov. 5, 1892.

Messrs. Effingham Maynard & Co.,
771 Broadway, New York.

Gentlemen,—Please send me by mail the following "English Classics":—

2 Brown's Rab and His Friends.
1 Swift's Gulliver's Voyage.
1 Scott's Lady of the Lake.

I inclose a money order for fifty cents.

Yours respectfully,
Nathaniel Rice.

What to See and Do.—Copy and describe this letter.

Write another order, in your own name, for Dickens's "Cricket on the Hearth," Irving's "Discovery of America by Columbus," and Parton's "Heroes of the Revolution."

LESSON CLI.—Business Letter.

Dover, Del., Oct. 3, '91.

Messrs. Gilman, Stewart & Co.,
Baltimore, Md.

Gentlemen,

Please send me by the Adams Express

5 yds. Velvet, Sample No. 2.
9 yds. Silk,   "   " 3.

Inclosed please find a draft for thirty dollars ($30).

Respectfully yours,
(Miss) Margaret Kent.

What to See and Do.—Copy this letter.
Name and describe each part.
How does Miss Kent show these strangers that she is to be addressed as *Miss*, not *Mrs.* ?
Custom does not allow a title as a part of one's signature.
Notice that in a bill of goods the names of the articles begin with capitals.
Write to your grocer for—
   5 lbs. Java Coffee.
   3 doz. Florida Oranges.
   8 oz. Allspice.

LESSON CLII.

Business Letter.

What to Do.—Write to some bookseller and stationer for—
 2 quires of Billet Note-paper (sample inclosed).
 2 packages of Envelopes to match.
 1 doz. Falcon Pens.
 1 Robinson Crusoe, School Edition.
 1 Swiss Family Robinson, Cloth.
Request that the bill be sent to your father. Give full directions.

LESSON CLIII.

Business Letter.

Copy the following letter, and notice every part :—

2022 Central Av.,
Minneapolis, Minn.,
Dec. 21, 1893.

Publishers of
"The Youth's Companion",
Boston, Mass.

Gentlemen,— For the inclosed money order ($1 $\tfrac{75}{100}$) please send to my address "The Youth's Companion" for one year, beginning with January, 1894.

Yours truly,
Francis Bacon.

What to Do.—Write to *The Century Co.*, 33 East 17th Street, New York, for "St. Nicholas" ($3).

LESSON CLIV.
Informal Notes.

Dear Miss Arnold,

Please excuse my absence from school. Mother is ill this morning.

Will you kindly tell my brother what lessons I should study?

Very respectfully yours,
Jane Dodge.

"Brook Farm,"
Wednesday, April 6th.

What to See and Do.—Copy and describe this note.

Write to your teacher, telling about a little journey you are going to make.

LESSON CLV.
Informal Notes.

Copy the following notes, and tell how they differ from the preceding letter-forms :—

My dear Ned,
        On Saturday papa and I are going up Beaver Creek for a day's fishing. Will you go with us?
        Truly yours,
                Fred.

Monday, June 2 d.

Dear Mr. Crane,
        Will you excuse a short notice, and dine with us to-morrow at seven o'clock?
        Very sincerely yours,
                Ida Young.

"Seaview,"
        Tuesday morning, 8 o'clock.

LESSON CLVI.

Formal Notes.

Copy these formal notes, and tell how they differ from preceding note-forms and letter-forms :—

INVITATION.

Miss Dora Lee requests the pleasure of Miss Maud Burr's company on Thursday evening, July 12th, from five to ten o'clock.
10 Prairie Av.

ACCEPTANCE.

Miss Maud Burr has much pleasure in accepting Miss Dora Lee's kind invitation for Thursday evening, July 12th.
9 Ocean Av., July 3d.

REGRET.

Miss Maud Burr regrets that a previous engagement prevents her accepting Miss Dora Lee's kind invitation for Thursday evening, July 12th.

9 Ocean Av., July 3d.

What to See and Do.—In a formal note you speak of yourself as you would of another person. You also speak *of,* not *to,* your correspondent.

In writing such notes be careful not to change and say *I, my,* etc.; *you, yours,* etc.

Write a regret and give a reason different from the one in the model.

LESSON CLVII.

Formal Notes.

What to Do.—Write a formal note inviting some *Miss* or *Master* to a garden party or to dinner.

Write a "regret," with a reason different from those mentioned in the other notes.

ABBREVIATIONS.

Find in the preceding letter-forms abbreviations for *Michigan, Washington, North Dakota, Wyoming, Delaware, Maryland, Minnesota.*

Washington, the name of a city, should not be abbreviated. It is better not to abbreviate names of cities.

Find abbreviations for *Messieurs* (gentlemen), *and company, dollars, yards, number, pounds, dozen, ounces.*

LESSON CLVIII.

Heading, Salutation, and Complimentary Close.

EXERCISE.

China, Kennebeck Co., Me., Jan. 31, '93.

Indianapolis, Ind., 666 Hadley Avenue, 1890, March 25.

Aug. 7, '94, Meridian, Miss.

P. O. Box 115, Topeka, Kans., Feb. 28, 1892.

What to Do.—From the lines above arrange four Headings to illustrate the different forms given on pp. 80, 83, 143, 146, 231, 233, 234, and 236.

EXERCISE.

1. Sir,
2. Madam,
3. Dear Sir,
4. Dear Madam,
5. My dear Sir,
6. Dear Miss Field,
7. Dear Mrs. Wood,
8. My dear Mr. Gray.

1. Yours truly,
2. Truly yours,
3. Very truly yours,
4. Sincerely yours,
5. Very sincerely yours,
6. Cordially yours,
7. Most cordially yours,
8. Ever faithfully yours.

What to See and Do.—Notice that the forms at the beginning of each list are for strangers, and that those farther on are for acquaintances and friends.

The Salutation and the Complimentary Close should be fitted to each other. You would not begin a letter with *Sir*, and close with *Ever faithfully yours*.

Select four forms of Salutation, and find for each a suitable Complimentary Close.

Show the proper position for these, using a line to represent the Body of the Letter.

Examine the letters and letter-forms given in your book, and describe the Salutations and forms of Complimentary Close.

LESSON CLIX.

Body of the Letter and Signature.

Hints.—Do not begin a letter with such unnecessary words as, "I now take my pen in hand," or "I now sit down to write you a few lines."

Let letters to friends be easy, "talking letters," giving information that you think will be most welcome.

In business letters, get directly at your work. State your points very clearly, and arrange them orderly.

In replying to a letter, acknowledge its receipt, and be careful to answer all its questions.

Signatures should be very plain.

Do not sign pet names in writing to strangers or mere acquaintances.

Titles are not used with Signatures, but a lady may put *Miss* or *Mrs.*, inclosed in curves, before her name, to show a stranger how she is to be addressed.

If the Heading of your letter does not show where you wish the answer sent, write your directions under your Signature, thus—

James Russell Johnson,
Englewood, N. J.

Or your directions may be given at the bottom of your letter, thus—

Please direct the answer to
Shelby,
Cleveland Co., N. C.

EXERCISE.

Your most welcome letter reached me _____

_____ .

You will, I am sure, be happy to hear _____

_____ .

Your kind favor of May 30th was duly received _____

_____.

What to Do.—You may add other lines to the three letters here begun, and use with each a Salutation, a Complimentary Close, and a Signature, to illustrate what has been taught.

Get what hints you can from the different forms in your book.

LESSON CLX.

Address and Superscription.

Hints.—The Address of the one written to is generally given at the head of a business letter. It is commonly omitted from familiar letters. If, however, a letter is important, this "inside address" should appear, as an element of safety.*

It is the same as the address on the envelope.

The address on the envelope is called the *Superscription.*

Pet names or nicknames should not be used here.

The Superscription should be put on the envelope neatly and tastefully.†

---

* Letters are sometimes opened by the wrong person, and the envelopes destroyed. A letter may be lost after being taken from the envelope. These and similar accidents could be remedied by the address in the letter.

† Many prefer to omit punctuation after the different parts of a Superscription. These parts, it is said, are sufficiently separated by their position.

The same reason could be given for omitting punctuation after the Saluta-

Have the open edge of your envelope from you when you write, or your Superscription will be upside down.

Put your stamp, right side up, on the upper right-hand corner, leaving a small margin around it.

EXERCISE.

The Rev.
  Asa J. Hodge, D.D.,
    Yankton,
      S. Dak.

Master Samuel Ames,
  Care of Abram Ames, Esq.,
    Virginia City,
      Nev.

  Mr. Edgar E. Clay,
    Leesburg,
      Va.
Loudoun Co.

---

tion, after the Complimentary Close, at the end of a paragraph, and in many other instances where custom requires its use.

We think it better to let the pupils use the comma and the period on envelopes as elsewhere, to prevent confusion, if for no other reason.

Rev. Mr. Hawthorne, Birmingham, Ala., P. O. Box 80.

Miss Flora T. Lyon, 22 Peachtree St., Atlanta, Ga.

Mrs. David B. Dana, 99 Boulder Av., Helena, Mont.

Dr. Morgan P. Gray, Odd Fellows Building, Portland, Oreg.

Prof. Clarence Cox, 776 Logan Av., Denver, Colo.

Messrs. Seth S. Scott & Co., Cooper, Delta Co., Tex.

Benjamin F. Blake, Esq., Phenix, Kent Co., R. I.

What to See and Do.—Review what is said about addresses, titles, etc., Lessons XXXII., XXXIII., XXXIV., XXXV., LXXIII.

Examine the Superscriptions given on pp. 82, 85, 144, 148, 231.

Draw the outlines of envelopes, and write the ten addresses above in the form of Superscriptions.

In the three preceding lessons find the abbreviations for *Maine, Indiana, Mississippi, Kansas, New Jersey, North Carolina, South Dakota, Nevada, Virginia, Alabama, Georgia, Montana, Oregon, Colorado, Texas, Rhode Island, post office.*

LESSON CLXI.

Friendly Letter.

What to Do.—Write to a friend, and express your thanks for an offer to lend you books.

You may say that you would like to read "Five Little Peppers, and How They Grew," by Margaret Sidney; "Alice's Adventures in Wonderland," by Lewis Carroll; and "Doings of the Bodley Family," by Horace E. Scudder. Tell your friend what books you will offer in return.

LESSON CLXII.

Business Letter.

What to Do.—Write to Messrs. Harper and Brothers, Franklin Square, New York City, and ask them to change the address of your "Harper's Young People." Give your old address and your new address.

In the same letter order "Harper's Magazine" ($4) and "Harper's Bazar" ($4). Have them sent to different persons. Give each address in full.

LESSON CLXIII.

Friendly Letter.

What to Do.—Write to a member of your family and describe a real or imaginary journey through important places.

If you have not taken the journey, learn from the geography or from your friends what you can about the places.

LESSON CLXIV.

Friendly Letter.

What to Do.—Write from some city and invite a friend living in the country to spend the Christmas holidays with you.

Tell what sights and entertainments your city will offer.

To the Teacher.—Letter-writing will be the only form of composition practiced by a majority of your pupils after they leave school.

The importance of this subject is evident.

Much care should be taken to cultivate neat, tasteful habits in all the forms and details of this work.

Additional Lessons.

Various subjects will present themselves for additional work in letter-writing.

To give an orderly account of the events of the day or the week ; or a special account of a day by the sea, a day in the mountains, a day on the farm, a visit to the city, an excursion, a picnic, a pleasant walk, etc., will make profitable exercises.

Dictation — Reviews.

The letters and letter-forms given for models may be written from dictation till the pupils learn the forms perfectly.

Frequent and thorough reviews should be given.

Outlines of Stories for Compositions.

LESSON CLXV.

Two Wise Goats.

1. Two goats meet on a narrow ledge.
2. A steep rock and a deep chasm.
3. One goat lies down.
4. The other passes over him and bounds away.
5. Suppose they had quarreled.

LESSON CLXVI.

The Strength of a Kind Word.

1. A heavily loaded cart.
2. The whipping of the horse.
3. His former master. "Come, Bob!"
4. The horse's look. "Anything for you."
5. Started the load, trotted on briskly.

LESSON CLXVII.

BE CAREFUL ABOUT SMALL MATTERS.

" For want of a nail the shoe was lost.
For want of the shoe the horse was lost.
For want of the horse the rider was lost.
For want of the rider the battle was lost.
For want of the battle the kingdom was lost."

LESSON CLXVIII.

THE SAILOR AND THE BIRDS.

1. *An English sailor freed from a French prison.*
2. *Met a bird-dealer on London Bridge.*
3. *Bought all the birds.*
4. *Opened the cage door.*
5. *Dealer scolded, sailor laughed.*
6. *" If you had been a prisoner——"*

LESSON CLXIX.

OBEYING PROMPTLY.

1. *A switchman's boy playing between the rails.*
2. *In danger from two approaching trains.*
3. *To go to his rescue would cause a collision.*
4. *Father shouted, " Lie down!"*
5. *Boy was accustomed to obey promptly. Saved.*

LESSON CLXX.

Taken at his Word.

1. A punctual merchant gave a mechanic an order for work.
2. "Will be done Thursday if I am living."
3. Did not come. Man's death put in the paper.
4. Man goes to printer.
5. Is sent to merchant. Surprised to see man alive.

LESSON CLXXI.

A Proud Corporal Punished.

1. Soldiers raising a heavy beam.
2. The Corporal shouts, but gives no help.
3. A man asks why. "I am a Corporal."
4. The man lifted with the soldiers.
5. Good day, Mr. Corporal. When help is wanted again, send for Washington.

LESSON CLXXII.

The Lion and the Mouse—A Fable.

1. A lion is sleeping. A mouse wakes him.
2. The mouse begs for his life. "May do you a kindness some time."
3. The lion, caught in a net, roars. The mouse gnaws the ropes.
4. Small things may be worth attention.

LESSON CLXXIII.

The Blacksmith's Shop.

1. *Describe the blacksmith.*
2. *His work.*
3. *Fire, bellows.*
4. *Anvil, hammer, tongs, water-trough.*
5. *The children coming home from school.*

LESSON CLXXIV.

A Noble Man.

1. *The bridge at Verona swept away.*
2. *People on the middle pier.*
3. *The Prince offered a large sum of money.*
4. *A young workingman seized a boat, and rescued the people.*
5. *"Here is your money." "I do not sell my life."*

LESSON CLXXV.

The Three Coachmen.

1. *An elderly gentleman advertised for a coachman. Three men came.*
2. *"How near can you drive to the edge of a precipice?" "Within an inch."*
3. *"How near can you drive?" "Within half an inch; have done it often."*
4. *"Well, my man, how near—?" "Never tried; shouldn't care to." "You're the sort of man."*

LESSON CLXXVI.

The Carpenter's Shop.

1. Work.
2. Bench, planes, chisels, hammers, mallets, adz, gimlets, saws, rule.
3. Compare blacksmith and carpenter.

LESSON CLXXVII.

The Wind and the Sun—A Fable.

1. Dispute which is stronger.
2. Which can first make a traveler take off his cloak.
3. The wind blew furiously. The traveler held his cloak tighter.
4. The sun shone. The traveler threw off his cloak.
5. Kindness often better than force.

LESSON CLXXVIII.

Cruelty to Animals.

1. Animals can feel.
2. How would you like the treatment?
3. "Do unto others——"
4. Story to show that animals are sometimes grateful.